PROBLEM OF SELF-RESPECT AND FOUR PERSPECTIVES

SARAKANAM SRINIVAS

To

My Father

Late Shree. SARAKANAM JAGANNADHAM

and

My Mother

Late Smt. SARAKANAM LAKSHMI

Contents

Preface

Abraham Lincoln stated that the Civil War, in fact, started with Harriet Beecher Stowe's novel Uncle Tom's Cabin, which had shaken the then American society and ushered in discussions and debates on the existing inhuman practice of slavery. The novels like Ananda Math of Bankim Chandra Chatterjee, Bharathi of Sarath Chandra etc., also ushered in severe discussions in the pre-independent era of India. Indira Parthasarathy's novel The River of Blood brought the massacre of Dalits to public notice in India. Society and literature are dialectically related, influencing each other. Some writings in specific historical contexts would influence the then-contemporary societies.

In his world renowned historical novel Spartacus, Howard Fast wrote that the legendary folk hero Spartacus (the leader of enslaved people who defeated the mighty Roman army in five battles) was inspired by the poems of Homer's Illiad. Every subject for every writing is taken from the social history only. In other words, socio-economic, political and cultural aspects reflect the confluence of fiction in the literature of any genre. It is with this idea, the current topic, Problems of the Dalits in Select Novels of Indian English: An Analysis of the Relationship between Society and Literature with reference to G. Kalyana Rao's Untouchable Spring, Mulk Raj Anand's Untouchable, Sivakami's The Grip of Change, and Bama's Sangati (Events) is chosen for study and analysis.

Dalits are marginalized in the caste-ridden Indian society. Though the Scheduled Castes and Scheduled Tribes (Prevention of Atrocities) Act 1989 came into practice, the atrocities on the Dalits have been conducted unhindered. In July 1998, in the Dholapur district of Rajasthan, a Dalit youth's nostril was forcibly pierced, and a string was drawn. It was later paraded around the village with an undue and vainglorious allegation that "herefused to sell 'bidis' (hand-rolled cigarettes) on credit" to the relative of the village head. In the same year, another shocking incident occurred in which the highly educated and responsible persons were involved with an age-old religious dogma. The High Court Judge of Allahabad in July 1998 got his chamber purified with the water of Ganga as it had earlier been occupied by a Dalit Judge. Another example of the oppressive and inhuman customs prevalent in India is the one that takes place as part of the worship of Deity. The caste Hindus, during the Marama village festival in Karnataka, force the Dalits to sacrifice buffaloes and drink their blood and run into the fields barefoot. Though there is a considerable decrease in the frequency of the occurrence of such incidents, the physical and mental assaults on the Dalits have not yet been entirely curbed. As the problems of exploitation and oppression as such are reflected in the select novels of this thesis, the choice of the subject is apt and relevant to the present history.

G. Kalyana Rao's Untouchable Spring is themed around the depressed and miserable lives of Dalits, narrating a hundred-year history of Dalits in Telugu society. It mainly focuses on the social and cultural oppression of Dalits. In this novel, G. Kalyana Rao mainly depicts how the Dalits are stigmatized in the socio-economic-cultural arenas in India. G. Kalyana Rao wrote Antarani Vasantam in Telugu in 2000. It was translated into English with the title Untouchable Spring in 2010 by Alladi Uma and M. Sridhar.

Being published in 1935, Mulk Raj Anand's Untouchable is a sociological novel that seeks to denounce the evil practice of untouchability by focusing attention on the dreadful conditions of a large section of Indian society. The theme of the novel Untouchable, a vigorous piece of social criticism, is concerned with the nonsensica practice of untouchability. M.R. Anand, in this novel, has portrayed the humiliations that happened in a day of the life of a sweeper boy whose character represents all the depressed people of India in the pre-independence era.

Sivakami's The Grip of Change deals with the problems of Dalits and the female subjugation and marginalization within the

Dalit community in the existing patriarchy. She translated her Tamil Pazhaiyana Kazhithalum in 1989 and Asiriyar Kurippu in 1997 into English with the title The Grip of Change and Author's Notes in 2006. However, the title which appears on the cover page is The Grip of Change as the Author's Notes is a mere explanation of her ideas expressed in The Grip of Change. The social relations and

the nature of grassroots level politics in the rural society of Tamil Nadu are skillfully brought before by the author in this novel. Bama's Sangati, initially written in Tamil in 1994, was translated into English by Lakshmi Holmstong in 2005. Bama's novel deals with gender oppression and caste-based discrimination that predominantly exist in society. She exposed the countless problems of the Dalit women who are doubly marginalized in the caste-ridden patriarchal society in this novel. This novel narrates how dalit women are subjugated by the unequal caste system and oppressive patriarchy.

As the focus of the research is the study and analysis of the problems of Dalits reflected in the select novels, the dialectical and historical materialistic method is employed. It is with this method that one can trace out the underlying relationship between society and literature. The entire thesis is written in seven chapters. While the first chapter constitutes "Introduction: Scope and Methodology", the history of Dalits with the same title is briefly discussed in the second chapter, followed by analyzing the four novels in the four successive chapters. Various similar and contradictory aspects and the different perspectives of the authors are analyzed in the seventh chapter, "Four Novels: An Assessment and A Proposition", which is followed by "Glossary" "works Cited".

About The Book

This book was a doctoral thesis by Dr Sarakanam Srinivas. He was enrolled for PhD (Part-Time) with Andhra University in October 2010 under the guidance of Dr Manjula Davidson, Professor, Department of English, College of Arts and Commerce, Andhra University Visakhapatnam, Andhra Pradesh, India. In November 2016, he submitted it for adjudication with the title, Problems of the Dalits in Select Novels of Indian English: An Analysis of the Relationship between Society and Literature. After three adjudications and subsequent viva voce, he was conferred on a doctorate on 7 July 2018. This thesis, with a few necessary minor modifications, is brought before the readers and researchers, now.

The author attempted to study the problems of the Dalits reflected aesthetically in the select novels of Indian writings in English by employing the dialectical and historical materialistic method. The dialectical relationship between society and literature was traced in this book. While society (social phenomena) forms the basis for the production of literature, literature, one of several social institutions, causes changes in society. With this basic understanding, the chosen texts were interrogated, analysed and assessed. The author's attempt to synthesise the ideas of Marx and those of Ambedkar is noteworthy in this book. This book would indeed interest researchers and those in social activism though the Marxist method was employed by the author with his then-limited understanding.

Sincere acknowledgements to www.niludamle.com, https://en.wikipedia.org/wiki/Periyar, and m.facebook.com/Savitribai-Phule from which the cover page pictures were taken.

Dr Sarakanam Srinivas

Associate Professor

Department of English

KLEF (deemed to be University)

Vaddeswaram, Guntur District

Andhra Pradesh, India
sarakanam.srinivas@yahoo.co.in
sarakanam.srinivas@kluniversity.in

Introduction

Scope and Methodology

The historical and contemporary social milieux are reflected in literature as the literature is created by man and the themes of literary texts --either poetry or prose, or any literary or non - literary piece of work-- are derived from the past or/and the then-contemporary history of society. The novels Untouchable Spring, The Grip of Change, Untouchable and Sangati (Events) reflect the miserable living conditions of Dalits, who are the marginalized in the caste-ridden Indian society. Various aspects of the lives of Dalits – social, economic, cultural, political and spiritual aspects-- have been recorded with from the perspective of resistance and protest in Indian literature. There is a dialectical relationship between society and literature. While society (social phenomena) forms the basis for the production of literature, literature causes changes in society.

In the novel, Uncle Tom's Cabin, the famous American writer Harriet Beecher Stowe portrayed the heartrending socio-economic conditions under which the slaves were living in America and how they were subject to the plundering exploitation and cruel disintegration of the slave families -- the members of the slave families were sold like commodities in the market, and therefore the intimate family relations were sabotaged, and the members of the family were scattered hither and thither-- by their white-masters. Having shaken the foundations of constitutional slavery that had been in practice in the then American society, this novel evoked sympathy in the hearts of people on the miserable living conditions of the slaves. It caused ushering in discussions and debates on slavery, a dreadfully severe problem of the day. The intensity of this socio-economic crisis and the significance of this novel were reflected in the statement made by the then President Abraham Lincoln that "the civil war, in fact, started with the novel, Uncle Tom's Cabin". This is a specimen of how literature causes societal transformation. Besides reflecting the then unjustifiable American social milieu, the novel Uncle Tom's Cabin caused a progressive change in society. The novels like Bankim Chandra Chaterjee's Ananda Math, Sarath's Bharathi also ushered in serious discussions in the educated circles of the day in India. Indira Parthasarathy's novel The River of Blood made the people aware of the Keezhavenmani massacre that took place in Tanjavur district of Tamil Nadu in 1968 and impelled the intellectuals to voice against the atrocities of the dominant on Dalits across the nation. Every literary work is not expected to bring in a new change in society, while every social incident is not necessarily the one that would be reflected in literature. Some writings in specific historical contexts would influence the then - contemporary societies.

Dalits, who have no place in the casteist Hindu religion based upon the four-Varna system, do not belong to any Varna. According to Manu Dharma, the Brahmins were born of the head of God, the Kshatriyas, the shoulders, the Vaishyas, the thighs and the Shudras, the feet and therefore Dalits, the so-called untouchables, had no scope to be born from any part of the body of God. This aspect of social discrimination reminds us of the words of the character of a little African American slave girl in the novel Uncle Tom's Cabin that "she [I] was never born".

Who Are Dalits?

A Dalit is a human being who is suppressed and oppressed and mercilessly thrown away to the lowest rung of society's hierarchical ladder (social structure). A person who is honest, wise and exceptionally talented in his chosen field may also become a socially underprivileged individual if he was born in a so-called untouchable family. Dalits are the marginalized in the Indian casteist society. However, the Dalit Panthers movement that emerged in the 1970s as a response to the atrocities being conducted on the down-trodden declared that besides all the depressed, the women of all castes are considered Dalits.

The Depiction of the Lives of Dalits in Indian Writings Madara Chennaiah, a 'cobbler – saint' who lived in the 11 th century A.D., during the regime of Western Chalukyas, was one of the first Dalit writers and considered the "father of Vachana poetry". The term "Dalit Literature"was firstly used in 1958 in the first conference of Maharastra Dalit Sahitya Sangh [Maharastra Dalit Literature Society] that was held in Bombay [Now Mumbai]. In this conference, Dalit scholars opined that the Dalit literature has to discuss all the aspects of caste to uproot it from Indian society and protest the discrimination and oppression unleashed on Dalits to establish alternative humane and democratic human relations in society. So, the literature which is produced for the emancipation and development of Dalits is called Dalit literature.

While the literature created by Dalits emphasizes the aspect Dalits' self–respect, the literature produced by non - Dalits sympathizes with them. The Telugu Dalit – Bahujan writer B. S. Ramulu opines:

> *"The literature which Dalits create is like a woman who experiences her labour pains, while the literature produced by non – Dalits is like a husband who stands outside feeling the pains of his wife. However, one need not be sceptic of the husband's emotional state of mind. Similarly, one need not be sceptic of the honesty and commitment of the non – Dalit writers (Prasad. 2000. P. 6)."*

Though Unnava Lakshmi Narayana, Mulk Raj Anand, Munshi Premchand, Rabindranath Tagore, Mahaswetha Devi and so on are the non – Dalit writers, they depicted the problems of Dalits in their writings in a heartrending way. Several saints like Swami

Ramananda, Sri Chaitanya, Basaveswara (Basava), Nanak, Kabir and so on protested the caste system and created Dalit literature during the phases of the Bhakti movements. In Telugu, Palkuriki Somanna, the follower of Basava (the 12 th century social reformer), Yogi Vemana, who worked for the eradication of the caste discriminations, Potuluri Veerabrahmam garu, who worked against the evil of untouchability closely moving with the Dalits and Tallapaka Annamayya, who expressed his dissent against the discriminatory caste system his verse in the realm of spirituality voiced against the caste discriminations and untouchability in the then-contemporary societies.

In the modern age, the great Telugu poets, Gurram Joshuva and Gurajada Appa Rao wrote against this social malady. Mahatma Jyothi Rao Phule, who denounced the Hindu Varna system through his movements and writings, opined in his book Gulamgiri that the ancestors of today's Dalits fought valiantly against the Aryan invasions. Consequently, the Aryans who were victorious made them untouchables through social eviction. Through his anti - Brahmanist movements and writings, Jyothi Rao Phule became a source of inspiration for B. R. Ambedkar and the other Dalit writers and activists. B. R. Ambedkar stated that Gautama Buddha, Kabir and Jyothi Rao Phule were his Gurus [philosophers and inspirers].

Even though several saints and activists produced (i.e., creative production) the Dalit literature, it is B. R. Ambedkar who studied deeply and produced a vast literature. Kalekuri Prasad, the eminent Dalit writer brings before people the literary contribution of several writers to the enrichment of the arena of Dalit literature. Inspired by the writings of Ambedkar, the Dalit Panthers movement was started. Arjun Dangle, Namdev Dhasal, J. V. Pawar, Anna Bau Sathe, Sankar Rao Karath, Babu Rao Bagul, Daya Pawar, Thrayambak Saskal, Avinash etc., emerged as literary personalities (Prasad. 2000). Being Dalits, they intensely expressed their personal experiences and emotions emanated from their injured hearts in their writings demanding the establishment of an egalitarian society in India.

Also, several Dalit and non – Dalit writers in Telugu wrote on the Dalit issue. Kalekuri Prasad further explains how the problems of Dalits were dealt with by various writers in Telugu. He says that "In 1913, Tallapragada Suryanarayana wrote the novel Helavati, while Venkata Parvatisam poets wrote Matru Mandiram in 1919. Unnava Lakshminarayana, in 1922 wrote the novel Malapalli which produced tremors in the hearts of British imperialists. N. G. Ranga's Harijana Nayakudu , Adavi Bapiraju's Narudu were published in 1936. In 1950, Vattikota Alwaru Swami's Prajala Manishi, in 1962, Muppalla Ranganayakamma's Bali Peetham were published. Dasarathi Rangacharya's Chillara Devullu (1970), Illendula Saraswati Devi's Neebanchen Kalmokta (I am your slave; I touch your feet, 1976), Akkineni KutumbaRao's Soraajjem (Freedom, 1984), Dadala Chantabbai's Antuleni Amavasya (1984) were also among the prominent Dalit writings. The Dalit writers like Gurram Joshua, Jala Rangakavi, Kusuma Dharmanna, Nakka China Venkaiah, Boyi Bheemanna, Gnyanananda etc., wrote on the problems of Dalits during the freedom movement" (Prasad. 2000).

Several Dalit writers have made literature a tool to sensitize society about the problems of Dalits. Some of them have written autobiographies to expose the cruel socio-economic discriminations which they miserably underwent. Om Prakash Valmiki's Joothan: A Dalit's Life and Narendra Jadav's Out Caste: A Memoir is the autobiographies that lay bare the oppression on Dalits in Indian society wherein the discriminative caste system has still been existing unhindered.

Revealing his personal experiences in his Joothan, Om Prakash Valmiki narrates the frustration and pain in his life caused by the supremacy of the upper castes. He attempts to lay bare the worthlessness of the outdated social system in which the individual is discriminated against based on his caste in his Joothan.

In his Outcaste: A Memoir, Narendra Jadhav explores the world he has lived in through the eyes of the members of his family. It, being an autobiographical fiction, attempts to help the readers make out the cruelty and injustice of the unequal hierarchical social order that treats a section of people derisively and inhumanly.

Namdev Dhasal, who is one of the founder leaders of the Dalit Panther Movement and well-known activist poet in Marathi literature, makes the readers aware of the widespread social evils like injustice, atrocities, inequality, poverty, and the violation of human rights and presents the tragic plight of the depressed in society by his poetry. His writings are a testimony that he favours socialism. He believes that poverty is the root cause behind the oppression of Dalits at the hands of the upper caste people. According to Dhasal, "the
unequal distribution of wealth has given certain sections of society the privilege to enjoy power and wealth while the deprived are forced to lead miserable lives" (Agarwal. 2010). He further mentions that the real struggle is to take place between the two classes --the rich and the poor. His poetry includes Golpitha, Moorkh Mhataryane [By A Foolish Old Man], Tujhi Lyatta Kanchi? [How Educated Are You?], Mi Marale Surya Chya Rathache Sat Ghode [I Killed the Seven Horses of the Sun], and Tujhe Boat Dharoon Mi Chalalo [I'm Walking, Holding Your Finger]. Besides two novels, Dhasal has published some pamphlets such as Andha Shatak [Century of Blindness] and Ambedkari Chalwal [Ambedkarite Movement]. His Ambedkarite Movement is a reflection on the socialist and communist concepts of Dr B. R. Ambedkar.

During the 1960s, a few writers like Anna Bhau Sathe, Shankar Rao Kharat, Bandhumadhar and so on wrote short stories with the inspiration of Dr B.R. Ambedkar. They depict the most tragic plight of the depressed in their writings. Their troubles and tribulations become the subject matter to be expressed through their stories. They could sensitize the people but are unable to make them ready to work for social change.

Baburao Bagul's writings reflect the anguish of the hearts of the section of people he belonged to. The purpose of his literary work is to rouse justifiable humane feelings among people regardless of their social identity. He firmly believes that the root cause of all pain is exploitation, and in his stories, several characters are victimized by exploitation. The Devadasis, sex workers, women of lower castes who are subject to sexual abuse, the men who are exploited just because of their lower caste etc., are the subject matter for him. He has portrayed the harsh reality of grimy slums, the ethical and unethical actions of the dwellers in the compelling situations of life. Unlike the heroes of the traditional type bearing the burden of their caste silently, the protagonists of Baburao Bagul are courageous to raise their voice against the oppressive social system.

The horrendous aspects of the caste system and the basis for the behavioral perversions are simultaneously explored in Vijay Tendulkar's play Kanyadaan. Tendulkar tries to justify the argument that "neurotic disorders born out of caste and religion-based ideology is an unacknowledged revelation of the discontent of civilization" (cited from Agarwal ed. 2000). In this play, the protagonist, being a scavenger by caste and because of his burden of caste, becomes a sadist and rebel.

Dalit consciousness is expressed in Rabindranath Tagore's play Chandalika also. Chandalika is a severe protest against untouchability and a true illustration of the consequences of the practice of suppression of individuals in the name of caste. The nature of the protest in Chandalika becomes more vehement because it is a resistance against the supremacy of patriarchy and Brahmanistic chauvinism.

Mulk Raj Anand expresses his deep-felt anguish through his novels and short stories, supporting the downtrodden and Dalits. His Untouchable and The Road deal with the problems of Dalits. He describes the pitiable and detestable living conditions of Dalits in his The Road. He rejects the "myth of sinful origin and condemns it as a manipulated design of corrupt Brahmins". In his The Village, he reveals the real account of the miserable conditions of the sweepers who are destined to take a breath in the most obnoxious and stinking odour.

In Seven Summers, Anand presents a stressful account of the

outcaste colony which is full of filth and dirt.

Expressing his grief over the caste-based discriminations in society, Raja Rao gives his voice to those who are weak and powerless in his story Javani. The theme of Javani deals with the misery in the life of Javani, a low caste woman who is subjugated for three reasons – first, for being a woman, second, for being a Dalit and third, for being a victim of poverty. Javani as a Dalit protagonist represents the women who accept their miserable lives as the predestined, assuming that it would be an offence to cross the drawn lines. In Javani, Raja Rao deals with the problems of Dalits, ignoring the necessity to struggle for political and social reform. He expresses his sympathy and love for Dalits, who accept the apathy of society with stoicism.

Girish Karnad, in his play Tale – Danda, voices against the discriminative caste system that has been in existence in society for ages. This play offers sufficient argument to lay bare the frightening horrors of caste politics in society. Voicing against untouchability and socio-economic inequalities in society, Mahasweta Devi, through her writings, hopes to sensitize the readers and audience about the socio-political issues related to the abandoned sections of society and wants to strengthen their struggle to attain the natural right of equality in society. Mahasweta Devi's Water is the story of a water deviner, Maghai, who is an outcast. The plot of the drama reveals his journey from "self-negligence to self-assertion" in which he becomes a leader of the depressed classes and starts to work for their social upliftment.

Premchand's short stories deal with various socio-economic problems and present a complete picture of the then society. The Shroud is a famous story of Premchand depicting the wretched conditions of Dalits. He shows in it how the traditional division of Varnas has affected the psyche of the marginalized class. His other short stories, The village well and Sadgati portray caste supremacy and depict how the upper castes exploit the lower caste people in the name of the caste backed by religion. His Sadgati reveals how Dalits are subject to boundless humiliation. On the one hand, it shows Brahminical hypocrisy, and on the other hand, it brings before us the miserable living conditions of Dalits.

Research problem statement

The sphere of Indian writings in English has been enriched with the contribution of several authors who penned on various grave issues that have been haunting the Indian marginalized sections for ages. Dalits are one such marginalized section in Indian society. Their problems were creatively reflected in the writings of the Indian literary trio –Mulk Raj Anand, R.K. Narayan and Raja Rao-- to current day writers. The present study tries to understand the problems of Dalits creatively reflected the select novels, tracing the relationship between society (material history) and literature (fictional episodes). It is necessary for one to know/enhance one's insight into the long-existing and long-troubling issue of Dalits' marginality and so this research contributes its part to the endeavors for the annihilation of the inhuman caste system.

Research questions

1. Are the problems of Dalits objectively reflected?
2. Can the relationship between society and literature be found conspicuously?
3. Can the impact of the authors' ideologies be traced in the themes, characterization and
4. narratives of their respective novels?
5. Do the select novels have any potential to bring qualitative change in society for the
6. resolution or at least the alleviation of the long-existing issue of the Dalit-marginality in
7. Indian society?

Research objectives

- To study the select novels distinguishing between fact and fiction.

- To investigate the historical authenticity of the fictional episodes.
- To understand the political inclination of the authors and analyze them accordingly.
- To identify the potential of the select novels whether they can contribute to progressive
- historical development.

The Scope of the Research

The study and analysis of the oppressed characters and the problems they undergo in their social life, how the characters of the marginalized are portrayed and how their problems are projected in these select novels; the political tendencies of the authors, and the exposition of the dialectical relationship between history (the material conditions of society, in other words the production relations) and literature are in the scope of the research.

The Method of Research

The study and analysis are carried out from the dialectical and historical materialistic perspective to achieve the aforementioned objectives. This method is also called the Marxist method propounded by Karl Marx and Frederick Engels. The analysis of art and literature from this perspective began with Karl Marx and Frederick Engels, followed by Plekhanov, Lunacharsky, Lenin etc., in the erstwhile USSR and Mao in the Peoples' Republic of China. Using the dialectical and historical materialistic perspective Rahul Sankrutyan wrote several historical novels in Hindi and analyzed several historical texts, both fiction and non-fiction, from Marxist perspective, while Debi Prasad Chatopadhyaya interpreted Indian philosophy from the same perspective. Varavara Rao worked on his doctoral research from the Marxist perspective and critically evaluated several literary works in Telugu. His analysis of several literary works i.e., the forewords he wrote to several texts were compiled and published with the title, Bhumiti Matadu: Fiction and Content Analysis. Using this method, Christopher Caudwell analyzed art and literature by tracing out the origin of poetry in his Illusion and Reality. Terry Eagleton discoursed various notions prevalent within the Marxist methodological framework in his Marxism and Literary Criticism.

According to Marxist literary criticism, the literary works are the creative reflections of various social institutions while the dynamics within them are the source/stimuli for the origin of literary works. Marxists believe that "literature itself is a social institution (as it can impact the human behaviour and action) and has a specific ideological function, based on the background and ideology of the author. One of the aims of Marxist literary criticism is to assess the "political tendency of a literary work, determining whether its social content or its literary form is progressive." Lunacharsky, one of the world-renowned exponents of the Marxist literary criticism, says:

> "*Marxist criticism is distinguished from all other types of literary criticism primarily by the fact that it cannot but be of a sociological nature – in the spirit, of course, of the scientific sociology of Marx and Lenin. ... For the Marxist critic, such a distinction [between literary critic and literary historian] loses nearly all its validity. Although criticism in the strict sense of the word must of necessity be a part of a Marxist's critical work, the sociological analysis must be an even more essential fundamental element.*
>
> *(Cited from "Theses on the Problems of Marxist Criticism". Trans. Y.Ganuskin. Source: A. Lunacharsky: On Literature and Art. Progress Publishers, 1973. Transcribed by Harrison Fluss for Marxists.org. Feb. 2008. Online.)*"

The production relations in various decades are reflected in these four select novels. The socio, economic, political, religious inequalities and gender oppression within and outside the family are reflected in a heartrending way in these novels. This research explores and traces the causes behind the maladies of the depressed depicted in the novels. Also, how these novels reflected the antagonistic contradictions between the ruling class and the ruled and the contradictions among the ruled are analyzed in this thesis. Aside from the above analysis, how these novels reflected the changes have taken place in the superstructure (social units) with the changes that have taken place in the base (production system). While the analysis of the relationship between the novels and the then-contemporary socio-political situation is the purpose of this research, it is equally imperative to achieve an insight into the same.

About Dialectical and Historical Materialism

Marxist philosophy i.e., the dialectical and historical materialism is an objective world outlook contrary to metaphysics. It helps people observe and understand the world explaining the cause and effect in every aspect. While matter is the basis for materialism, matter with motion is the basis for dialectical materialism because matter and motion are inseparable. Frederick Engels says:

"Dialectics is nothing more than the science of the general laws of motion and development of nature, human society and thought. (Anti - Duhring, by Frederick Engels, cited from the article An Introduction to Dialectical Materialism by Robin Clapp)."

Nature exists by itself. Nothing has separate existence in Nature. Everything is in existence being in relation with every other thing, either directly or indirectly. As everything is in motion, everything changes, and this change is both quantitative and qualitative. The quantitative changes lead to the occurrence of qualitative changes, and this change occurs abruptly. There are both internal and external causes for it. The role of the internal causes is crucial and the determiner, while the external causes (that exist in accordance with the internal causes) have their role. There is a struggle as well as unity between the opposites in Nature. It is this struggle that is the basis for change. Of the two opposite things, only one is the primary, and the other is secondary. The essence of an element/system is determined by the primary, while the secondary always tries to reach the level of the primary. The outlook and ideology of the primary (the ruling class) become the outlook and ideology of the secondary (the ruled) to the most extent.

The basis for ideas is the matter as they are born out of it. The brain using which we think is also matter. As Mao rightly says, ideas will not drop from the sky but sprout only from the social practice of man. Struggle for production, class - struggle, and scientific research are the bases for knowledge and ideology. When the observation and hypothesis result from social practice and stand for examination and experimentation, the hypothesis would become a scientific theory. Hence practice is the basis for ideas, and the role of ideas is significant in the development of society. When the people absorb the potent ideas to usher in change, they become a material force that determines societal transformation.

Dialectical materialism and historical materialism are inseparable. They are the living organs of Marxist philosophy. History is not something like compiling a few incidents that took place in a period or achievements of some individuals in the past; it is the struggle of people for their existence and the role they played in the development of society. Some laws govern social development, just as how Nature is governed by its laws.
J. V. Stalin says,

> *"Historical materialism is the extension of the principles of dialectical materialism to the study of social life, an application of the principles of dialectical materialism, to the phenomena of the life of society, to the study of society and of its history. (Dialectical And Historical Materialism, National Book Agency Private ltd. P 5.)"*

Social ideas, ideologies, political views, and political institutions are based on production relations which are also called the material conditions of social life. The ideas and ideologies born out of the existing material conditions influence the material conditions of social life. The evolutionary development of society takes place only through the conscious efforts of human beings. The result of such efforts occurs following specific laws of social dynamics but not according to the wishes of Man.

Production of basic needs is essential, and so a system of production is formed. The productive forces viz land, machines, labourers, etc., and the production relations together are called the production system. The relations formed between man and production and man and man in the production process are production relations or property relations, or social relations. This itself is the material life of human beings. It is this material life that the consciousness of men comes from. Hence, consciousness is determined by the material conditions of social life. As Karl Marx says:

> *"It is not the consciousness of men that determines their being; on the contrary, their social being determines their consciousness. (A Contribution to the Critique of Political Economy, pp 20-21. cited in Marxist philosophy: An Introduction, New Vistas Pub., New Delhi, 2002, p 131.)"*

While, according to historical materialism, the economic system of society is the base, religion, philosophy, politics, art, literature etc., are the peripheral aspects that constitute the super- structure. All these elements are the forms of social consciousness/ideology. The main cause for changes in consciousness is the occurrence of changes in the base, i.e., the economic system though it is not the only cause (i.e, the influence of the interaction between and/or among the superstructural elements is not to be belittled). There is a dialectical influence between the base and the super-structure. The same exists among the various aspects of the super-structure. The changes in the base come to the notice of human beings through their direct observation of the forms of social consciousness (superstructure). The development of productive forces takes place consistently as the development is a natural social phenomenon. This development will bring in change in the existing production relations. When the development of productive forces reaches a certain level, the old relations of production become a bottleneck to further progress of the productive forces. Then the development of productive forces moves ahead, destroying the old relations. This itself is a social change --Revolution. The development in productive forces reflects in the changes which take place in the relations of production.

Dialectical and Historical materialism – The Analysis of Literature

Literature, being a social institution, is a form of social consciousness. So, while studying or analyzing literature, we should do it considering the development in productive forces and the changes in the production relations of the day. The changes that occur in the production system and the way they are reflected in the super-structure that includes literature have an intimate relationship with one another. It is this relation that is to be taken into consideration. The production relations reflected in the literary texts are to be analyzed against the then-contemporary social conditions in which the stories of texts were set. In which historical phase and in what sort of production relations the author lived or lives and to which class the author belongs are to be essentially taken into consideration. How the contemporary production system in society reflects in literature is to be analyzed with the help of authentic and genuine data collected to assess the nature and worth of a particular literary work. Literature is always in compliance with the laws of social dynamics or development. B. Krylov Explains:

> *"Marx and Engels considered it absolutely impossible to understand art and literature proceeding only from their internal laws of development. In their opinion, the essence, origin, development, and social role of art could only be understood through the analysis of the social system as a whole, within which the economic factor – the development*

of productive forces in complex interaction with production relations—plays the decisive role. Thus art, as defined by Marx and Engels, is one of the forms of social consciousness, and it, therefore, follows that the reasons for its changes should be sought in the social existence of men. (Marx, Engels, On Literature, Progress pub., Moscow, 1978, p.17)"

Therefore, it is not a correct approach to study and explain the literary texts only by following the conventional principles of literature, such as those laid down in Poetics by Aristotle, some methods like 'Touch Stone' by Mathew Arnold, or the theory of depersonalization by T.S. Eliot and so on. So, the assessment of literary texts is to be done by studying the relationship between the literary elements and the then-contemporary production (social) relations. In Marxist understanding, according to the study of enotes, "literature, like all forms of culture, is governed by specific historical conditions, and that literature, as a cultural product, is ulitimately related to the economic base of society" (What are the main...2021). Hence, the dialectical and historical materialistic method is to be employed to carry out this research in accordance with the objectives set.

It is aimed to study and analyze the four chosen novels using this method. The social relations that existed in various decades of the 20 th century are reflected in the four select novels. The social, economic, political, religious inequalities, the gender oppression within and outside the family; the mal administration of the state-run machinery, the uncouth and heinous behaviour of government officials and the state violence on the depressed class, sexual exploitation of women workers, and so on, are depicted in a heartrending way in these novels.

This research also aims to analyze the problems of the depressed depicted in the select novels tracing the causes behind those problems. Also, how these novels reflected the antagonistic contradictions between the ruling classe and the ruled is also analyzed as part of this research. And how these contradictions are reflected not only in the economic sphere (the base) but also in the social, political and religious realms (superstructure) is also analyzed.

The analysis of the relationship between the novels and the then-contemporary socio-political history is the purpose of this research. In Marxist understanding, it is the literature of socialist reality that can reflect contradictions between and/or among classes in society and mobilize people for societal transformation. As the authors of these select novels (based on the preliminary understanding of the researcher) try to depict the material conditions of social life in the then-historical eras, standing in support of the depressed, it is reasonable, justifiable, and highly essential for the researcher to analyze these novels from the dialectical and historical materialistic perspective.

However, it is also essential for the researcher to assess the worth of the select novels whether they can bring progressive social change in society. The relationship between the novels and the production relations of the day (during which the stories of the novels were set) should be analyzed while analyzing the novels. Because, just as in Nature, nothing exists in isolation in society, too. The then-contemporary material conditions should be studied in the economic, social, political, and cultural realms. The interaction between and/or among all these elements are to be studied and analyzed objectively. Hence the analysis of the chosen literary texts begins with the study of the economic, socio-political and cultural conditions under which the marginalization of Dalits had its origin and its undue existence even in the new millennium.

CHAPTER TWO

Dalits In History

The term 'Dalit' means a person who is broken, crushed and destroyed. This term was firstly used in the nineteenth century by Mahatma Jyoti Rao Phule (1826 – 1890), a great social revolutionary. He used it to describe the outcasts as the oppressed and the broken victims of the caste-ridden Indian society. However, Dalit Panthers consider the term 'Dalit' to be a 'constant reminder of their age-old oppression, indicating both their state of deprivation and the oppressed people'.

Dalits, being called differently across the nation, have several names that include Asura, Avarna, Nishada, Panchama, Chandala, Dasa, Rakshasa, Harijan, Untouchable and so on. In addition to these names, several other names have been given to them regionally. They include Chura in Punjab, Bhangi in Hindi speaking states in North India, Mahar in Marathi, Mala, Madiga in Telugu, Parayan in Tamil and Paravan in Malayalam. Through the act of 1935, the British named them the depressed classes and the scheduled castes. Mahatma Gandhi called them Harijans, which means the children of Vishnu (God). Dalits are reluctant to be called so as the term Harijan does not describe their condition appropriately. B. R. Ambedkar openly stated that calling the Avarnas as Harijans is nothing but a great insult.

The Origin of outcasts: Some Theories

Gandhiji states that the caste system is a blot on the Hindu religion. The caste system, being a cruel social practice in India, categorizes human beings into different groups. Manu dharma, the

Hindu religious code of conduct, divides people into four Varnas, otherwise called castes. The institution of the caste system is a 'multifaceted exploitative cultural system'. This has been the main source of oppression and exploitation of Dalits for thousands of years. While the Brahmins occupy the top most place in the four-Varna system, the Kshatriyas are just below them. The Vyshyas are at the third rung of the hierarchical social ladder of the Varna system, while the Shudras are placed at the bottom rung. Besides these four caste divisions, there is yet another distinct social group of people in Indian society. Based on their so-called polluting nature, they are considered socially unworthy to be included in the caste system. They are the outcasts or the Avarnas. Constituting about 14% of India's population, they form a larger section without any caste identity in Indian society. Nevertheless, they do not constitute a separate society as they are an integral part of Indian society. Even though the outcasts are not part of the caste system, their lives are inextricably tied to the machine of the caste system. Their cultural identity, areas of habitation, social and marital relations etc., continue to be formed by the cultural aspects of the caste system.

The 'purity – pollution' principle in the caste system is quite unfair against Dalit communities. When the aspects like birth and death cause temporary pollution for Hindus, the religious ritual or simple bathing can restore a temporarily polluted person to the status of ritual purity. However, this is not the case with those who are permanently polluted as no purification rituals, bathing or cleaning acts can re- establish a permanently polluted person as pure. Dalits, in Hinduism, are regarded as permanently polluted people.

The people in India generally regard Dalits as polluted because of the kinds of jobs they engage in, such as skinning or removing animal carcasses, manual scavenging, leather work, drum beating, cremation work, toddy – tapping and so on. These are considered the polluting occupations as they deal with human waste and polluting objects.

In addition to this argument, there is another argument that is based on racial differences. Mahatma Jyoti Rao Phule opines that the native races of India valiantly fought the Aryans, who are the foreigners. Even though some native races obeyed the foreign rulers, the other races continued to fight the Aryans. Those who were strong and stubborn and did not like to lose their freedom and sovereignty were made untouchables by the Aryan rulers with the help of the priest class. This inhuman and discriminative ideology is deliberately imbibed into the minds of caste people for ages by the ruling classes. Thereby, the native people of this country have been made untouchables since then. However, B.R. Ambedkar opines in a different way saying that Dalits have been considered the untouchables because they eat cow meat, a sacred animal to Hindus.

> "*When the cow became sacred and beef-eating became taboo, society became divided into two — the settled community became a touchable community, and broken men became an untouchable community. (Ambedkar's Writings, vol . 7, p. 370)*"

Movements Against Untouchability

One of the foremost movements for eradicating the caste system and educating the downtrodden was the Lingyat movement led by Basavanna in the 12 th century in Anubhava Mantapa in Kalyani of Karnataka. The Vedas were rejected, and similar Vachanas were compiled. A large number of Dalits were attracted to the religion established by Basava in those days.

Swami Dayananda advocated that people are to go back to Vedic life. He exhorted that the Hindu nation should accept social reform like the abolition of untouchability, sati, dowry, etc. The religious reformers like Swami Vivekananda, Ishwara Chandra Vidhyasagar, Sri Aurobindo voiced against the oppressive and exploitative caste system, strongly condemning untouchability.

Mahatma Jyoti Rao Phule, who vehemently condemned the discriminative Hindu Varna system, established Satya Shodhak Samaj in 1873. He challenged the view that the Varna system was 'god–ordained' and publicly stated that the above claim was made to deceive the lower castes. Exposing the fallacy in the Hindu religious texts, he said that the 'highest rights and privileges' were given to the Brahmins in the Varna system. In contrast, the Shudras and the 'Atishudras' [Dalits] were regarded with hatred and contempt. He advocated that the lower castes and the 'untouchables' should unite against the supremacy of the Brahmins and strive for a justifiable society.

St. Narayana Guru led several social movements in Kerala against social inequalities and untouchability. Along with Periyar Erode Venkata Ramaswami Naiker, he led the Vaikom Satyagraha [a historic movement against the practice of untouchability] and succeeded in fetching some civil rights to the 'untouchables' in Vaikom, Kerala. He propagated the principles of rationalism, self–respect, women's rights and eradication of the caste system. He led the Vaikom Satyagraha and became famous as 'Vaikom Hero' in Tamil Nadu and Kerala.

Born in a Dalit Chamar family, B.R. Ambedkar fought for the liberation of Dalits from the cruel pangs of untouchability. He dedicated his life to this noble social cause. Having mobilized the Mahar caste people, he launched a temple entry movement in the year 1927. Between 1927 and 1935, he led three such movements. The vital movement of the three was the historic Mahad Satyagraha in 1927. This movement aimed to achieve equal rights for Dalits on Mahad freshwater tank (Choudar tank). He fought for separate electorates for untouchables and made the British government agree to it. However, he withdrew from his attempts when Gandhiji began a fast–unto–death against separate electorates.

Gandhiji, too, condemned the inhuman practice of untouchability. He called untouchables 'Harijans', which means the children of Vishnu [God]. With the 'blessings' of Gandhiji, Harijan Seva Sanghs were formed and campaigned against the practice of untouchability. Having denied the 'concept of high and low', he emphasized the division of labour through the caste system. Expressing his idea on caste and untouchability, he says:

"Untouchability is the product, therefore not of the caste system, but of the distinction of high and low that has crept into Hinduism and corroding it. The attack on untouchability is thus an attack upon this 'high – and – low – ness'. The moment untouchability goes, the caste system itself will be purified; that is to say, according to my dream, it will resolve itself into the true Varna dharma, the four divisions of society, each complementary of the other and none inferior or superior to any other, each as necessary for the whole body of Hinduism as any other. (Contextualizing Dalit Consciousness in Indian English Literature, Yking Books, Jaipur, 2010, P . 126)"

Other Major Incidents

In 1890 Gopal Baba Walankar established Anarya Dosh Parihar Mandali, intending to improve the socio-economic conditions of Dalits. Swami Sahajanandan from Madras organized the untouchables and claimed the right of access to the water of a tank at Omekalam in 1917. The Congress party, at its annual session held at Calcutta on 26 Dec 1917, passed a resolution against the age-old practice of untouchability. On 27 July 1918, Chhatrapati Shahu Maharaj of Kolhapur declared that "the untouchables in his state would be able to enjoy all the civil rights without any hindrance on the ground of untouchability". In 1922, the Madras Provincial legislative council passed a resolution recommending that Panchama and Pariah be replaced by Adi – Dravida and Adi – Andhra, respectively.

The Bombay legislative council on 4 August 1923 adopted the resolution that "the untouchable classes should be allowed to use all the public watering places, wells etc., which are built and maintained out of public funds". On 7 November 1933, Mahatma

Gandhi launched his countrywide tour to propagate against the evil practice of untouchability. From Wardha to Varanasi, he toured for nine months covering more than 20,000 kilometers addressing meetings, collecting funds and making the caste Hindus aware of the adverse effects of untouchability on Hindu society. On 19 March 1940, B.R. Ambedkar and his followers (about 15,000) celebrated 'Independence Day' of the depressed classes at Mahad.

On 29 April 1947, the Minorities and Fundamental Rights Committee of the Constituent Assembly decided that "untouchability in any form is to be abolished and the imposition of any disability on that account shall be an offence". The Constituent Assembly eventually passed this provision on 29 November 1948. The constitution of India, which came into implementation on 26 January 1950, provides under Article 17
as given below:

> *"Untouchability is abolished, and its practice in any form is forbidden. The enforcement of any disability arising out of untouchability shall be an offence punished in accordance with the law."*

The parliament of India had passed the protection of civil Rights Act, 1955, which came into force on 1 June 1955. This Act provides punishment for the offences committed on account of untouchability.

Although the anti – untouchability laws are enacted in the parliament, the practice of untouchability and oppression are not yet eliminated from Indian society. In response to this unjustifiable conditions, the Dalit Panthers movement arose in Maharastra in April 1972. This movement was organized under Namdev Dhasal, Raja Dhale Arun Kamble etc., and became popular in the 1970s and the 80s. The Dalit Panthers movement was entirely different from the earlier Dalit movements. Socio- political analysts comment, "Its initial thrust on militancy through the use of rustic arms and threats gave the movement a revolutionary tinge". This movement led to the emergence of several caste-based organizations and parties. The Bahujan Samaj Party [BSP] started to gain popularity among Dalits. Although Dalits form into organizations and political parties, they are still subject to harassment, violence and discrimination in India, especially in rural regions. The constitutional goal of Liberty, Equality and Fraternity have remained attained in India even after six decades of independence.

CHAPTER THREE

Untouchable Spring: A Novel Of Socialist Realism That Has Potential To Propel People For Constructing A New Humane Social Structure

G. Kalyana Rao's Untouchable Spring, originally written and published in Telugu in 2000, was translated into English in 2010 by Alladi Uma and M. Sridhar. This novel is an aesthetic record of the socio-economic, political and cultural problems of Dalits. The words "... there was a lot to be dug, a lot to be filled"(p. 80) are not the mere contextual words of a character but the author himself. He immerses himself in historical facts and presents them through fictitious scenes. His legitimately deep-felt anguish is reflected throughout the novel. Though the novel is mainly themed around the problem of self-respect and cultural identity, the issues related to basic amenities such as land, water, habitation etc., have not remained untouched.

The problem of Self Respect

The eminent philosopher and social activist Periyar E.V. Ramaswami Naiker opines that poverty can somehow be overcome if good opportunities are provided to the poor, but the untouchables cannot achieve equal social status in society unless there is a social revolution. B.R. Ambedkar states, "Untouchability is another appellation of slavery. No race can be raised by destroying its self-respect. So if you really want to uplift the untouchables, you must treat them in the social order as free citizens, free to carve out their destiny."The authour, G. Kalyana Rao too opines the same. However, he believes that the social revolution should be carried out through armed struggle.

Self-respect is one of the several aspects that G. Kalyana Rao dexterously deals with in Untouchable Spring. Dalits, who work in the fields and factories, are the true producers of wealth. Their contribution to the progress of society is enormous, so they are like the season of 'Spring' which symbolizes beauty and life. However, this Spring is untouchable to the touchable society. Speaking through the character of Ramanujam, the author scorns this social injustice: "Each one knows the greatness of his caste. If I am an untouchable to him, he's an untouchable to me too."(Untouchable Spring, p. 196). In fact, Yellaanna, the protagonist in the novel, leaves home unable to get an answer that could restore his people's self-respect. The author, G. Kalyana Rao, deals with self-respect in three contexts: When Dalits perform the street plays; when Dalits keep off eating the meat of dead cattle; and when the Harijan Sevak Sangh takes up a pseudo reformation programme. The question of self-respect begins in Yallanna's mind when he plans to perform a play in Dibbalamitta village.

The Performance of Street Plays

How the dominant suppress the downtrodden whenever the latter try to raise their heads to breathe the air of freedom with self-respect is shown through the street play episodes in this novel. The social relations under feudalism are based on the conception, "the superior dictate the inferior". Here, there is no scope for mutual respect between the superiors and the inferiors. While the superiors treat the latter with contempt, the inferiors are dictated to look at their masters with reverence. The individuals at the higher rung of the social hierarchy cannot tolerate the unity and amity among their inferiors. They wish that their inferiors should never raise their heads. If it happens so, the superiors will not hesitate to chop off those heads. Besides property, the superior class retain a self-centred nature and vainglory in their possession. However, these inhuman and dominating social aspects originate and are nurtured on the fertile field of exploitative property (production) relations. Hence, the underlying cause for the existence of such relations is the existing feudal production relations. This tyrannical attitude of the feudal lords and those of the surrounding villages have ruthlessly crushed the efforts of Dalits, who try to achieve self-respect by the act of respecting their caste elders before the beginning of the play.

Naganna prepares his men as actors to perform Bagotam, a street play. Bagotam does not remain as a mere play but a form of expression of self-respect as the Bagotam troupe is created and trained by themselves. The actors and spectators are malas and madigas, and the language of the dialogues in the play is informal and conversational. Watching the play, they can laugh freely and need not fear that an elder of the village would see, as it is their 'own' performance.

As the play is performed on the street of malas amidst the Dalit spectators, Naganna includes inviting and honouring pedda mala and pedda madiga to come and be seated at the beginning of the play. This act raises the self-esteem of Dalits. Until then, it had been a tradition that they would invite the Karanam or the other elderly men of the village. However, now Dalits begin to respect themselves. When Naganna begins to invite their elders, they are unable to believe their own ears. They are awe struck with Naganna's words. "Silence. The people wondered whether they had really heard the words they had. What did he say? Ah! Did he say that! The crowd was wonder – struck."(ibid. p. 75)

They watch the first performance with contentment, and they watch it freelywithout fear and inhibition. Later, at the request of people, they perform the play in Pakkela Dinni, Kolla Dinni and Chintalagunta. However, the newly introduced tradition, before the beginning of the play, causes furore in the village elders as it had until then been a convention for the narrator of the play to ask before the start of the

performance, 'Has the Karanamgaru come, have the Kapus come?' and only after their arrival the performance would begin. If any 'Reddy' comes late, the performance is to begin all over again.

Being intolerant of this new change, the upper caste elders of Yennela Dinni consider it an act of defying the long-established conventions. They cannot put up with the action of raising the mala and the madiga to the level of a karanam or a kapu or a reddy, and therefore they decide to 'teach a lesson' to them. They choose Dibbalamitta village as a battlefield for this.

Dibbalamitta Performance

In the Dibbalamitta episode, the writer shows how Dalits are deprived of self - respect due to the unjustly existing caste hegemony. Dibbalamitta is Atchireddy's in- law's village. Bukkireddy is Atchireddy's father – in – law who is 'an obstinate fool', is infuriated on hearing about the new change in the tradition of Yellanna's performance. He says, after his discussion with younger karanam and Atchireddy, "if it were me, I would kill those two bastards."(ibid. p. 79). These are not the mere hollow words that people generally utter while in an emotional state of frenzy. Landlords sometimes would really kill Dalits and the other lower caste people for trivial reasons just for satiating their ill-tempered ego. It happened more often under

feudalism. However, the same oppressive conventions have been in vogue even after independence, though the constitution provides equal rights to Dalits and lower castes on par with upper castes.

The day before the performance in Dibbalamitta, Bukkireddy warns the mala and madiga elders that both the mala and madiga palles [means an area adjoining the village] in Dibbalamitta would be 'turned into ashes' unless they withdraw the tradition of inviting of pedda mala and pedda madiga in the way the elders of the village are called on. The frightened Dalit elders ask the troupe to perform the play without respecting them and express their fear and anxiety, saying that they cannot live going against a landlord like Bukkireddy. It is true that Dalits cannot survive going against the upper caste landlords their pay masters, who may refuse to give them work in their fields or may set their huts ablaze or may even kill them. However, considering that self-respect is more important than performance, Naganna and Yellanna decline their appeal and tell them they would perform on some other day.

The threatening of Bukkireddy rouses a strong desire for self-respect in the mind of Yellanna. This incident has become the basis for his emergence as a folklorist. This makes him think of the problem of self-respect and realize that the issue of self-respect is not a small thing. This incident makes him understand that the upper cast chauvinism never allows the lowest of the lowly to raise their heads with self-respect. Unable to know what is to be done, he leaves home searching for the answer to help his race achieve self-respect.

Resistance to Keep off Eating the Dead Cattle

In his novel, G. Kalyana Rao depicts how tyrannically the upper caste landlords impose socio-cultural restrictions on Dalits. These imposed socio-cultural restrictions are both exploitative and oppressive. Though Dalits assume that eating dead cattle is their traditional right, the core of that tradition is economic exploitation. The caste Hindus do not eat the meat of the dead cattle but exchange the same with a pair of manufactured chappals [footwear].

Inviting the pedda mala and pedda madiga in the way the karanam and kapus are invited is banned. Similarly, when Dalits decide to keep off the eating of dead cattle, as an attempt to revive their self–respect, the village elders coerce them to eat it. Kalyana Rao explains it through Martin's experience. Martin realizes that the eating of dead cattle is inhuman, and therefore he wants it to change. Being a preacher, he mentions it during the prayer; they are surprised and worried to have listened to his words as they have been eating it for ages, and therefore, they think they cant avoid this custom. Listening to such words is too strange for them. Furthermore, when the caste elder says that accepting the dead cattle is their right, Martin discloses the treachery of the dominant. Ridiculing the argument of upper castes (that eating the meat of dead cattle is the right of Dalits), the writer here comments on the exploitative production relations in feudal societies through the character of Martin.

> *"The fields by the Krishna River were the right of the kammas. The fields by the Penna River were the right of the reddys. But there and here too, as for the dead cattle, they were the right of the madigas. He could not stop laughing. He laughed. He said even as he laughed. Finally, that palle said okay. They firmly decided they would not eat the dead cattle. (ibid. p. 161)"*

Having been inspired by the words of Martin, madigas decide to refrain from eating the dead cattle meat and this progressive act of madigas stokes up the anger of the village elders. When it comes up for discussion, all the landlords reach a conclusion that the madigas' decision is against their economic interests. If a madiga takes the dead cattle and its meat, he has to stitch slippers from the hide of the dead cattle for the person who gives his dead cattle, and if he does not eat the meat of the dead cattle, there is no question of slippers. In this context, this aspect has mirrored the feudal production relations between the upper castes and Dalits.

It is evident that while Dalits decide to abstain from the meat of dead cattle and live with self-respect, the upper caste lords become contemptuous at their decision. Contrary to this, the same caste Hindus put Dalits aside from the mainstream of social life, showing that Dalits eat the meat of dead cattle. This is an instance of paradoxical exploitative and discriminative social relations in feudal societies. This fact is reflected in the episode of China Jalaiah's dead bullock.

The Dead Bullock Incident

When the bullock of Venkayamma garu's China Jalaiah dies, Sinnenkadu and his son attend to this job. He skins the bullock and takes it, but later, he digs a pit and buries its bones and flesh. After taking its hide, the 'Choudaries' come to know that Sinnenkadu has buried the bones and flesh. Besides this, they also understand that the malas and madigas had not crowded at the dead cattle for meat just as they used to do earlier, surrounding the dead cattle with vessels quarrelling with one another. They demonstrate dignified manners by burying the flesh and bones of the dead cattle. However, this dignity of Dalits is not tolerated by village elders.

After the work is over, Sinnenkadu goes to Bucchi Choudary, who went to China Choudary's house. He goes there where many people who belong to the Choudary caste [an upper caste] assemble. When China Jalaih asks him when he would give slippers, Sinnenkadu replies that he has buried the bones and flesh, implicitly conveying that he does not have to make and give any slippers as he has not taken flesh. Bucchi Choudary, with his malicious interpretation, stokes up the fury of China Choudary. In a frenzy of excitement, China Choudary takes a long stick and begins to beat Sinnenkadu, abusing 'Eat the one you buried, you wretched bastard!'. Other elders also join hands with China Choudary in beating, and all of them chase Sinnenkadu to the outskirts of the village where he buried the cattle. They threaten him to take the dead body out, cook it and eat or else they would bury him in the pit itself. Later, they leave the spot 'as if they had preserved a great tradition' (ibid. p. 163) Through this episode, the author exposes the atrocities that are unleashed on Dalits in the feudal societies with impunity and how the landlords often resort to violence on the downtrodden is reflected in this context.

Harijan Seva Sangh and Purificatory Rituals

B.R. Ambedkar says, "There have been many Mahatmas in India whose sole object was to remove Untouchability and to elevate and absorb the depressed classes, but everyone has failed in their mission. Mahatmas have come, Mahatmas have gone, but the Untouchables have remained as Untouchables."The novel Untouchable Spring mirrors the above fact. As a counter to the pseudo reformation attempts of landlords, G. Kalyana Rao upholds the struggle for self-respect through the character of Ramanujam in a context. While talking with Reuben, Ramanujam ridicules the fake reformation of Gandhiji's followers who allow Dalits into temples but later, when the programme is over, they perform the purificatory rituals in the absence of Dalits. The double standards of Gandhiji's followers are admonished in this context. Though the upper castes do not allow Dalits to touch the lake water, they drink the water in the houses of Dalits for political gains. This grim social reality of the day is reflected in this context. The intense desire for retaining self-respect by Dalits is reflected through these episodes. Sometimes, the author himself is heard in the words of Martin who, when ridiculed the exploitative land relations in the then-contemporary society.

Art and Literature: The struggle for Identity

There are several artists – characters in this novel. Chandrappa, Naganna, Yellanna are the artists, while Yellanna is a folklore singer too. In addition to Yellanna, Bhudevi and Sasirekha are also singers. Potter Pedakoteswarudu is a poet, while Ruth is a writer. G. Kalyana Rao treats these characters in a lively manner. The author opines that the artistic and literary talent of the lower caste people has long been ignored, and therefore their talent has not been recorded in history. Kalyana Rao explains why the art of the oppressed has not got due recognition by the character Ruth:

"Unless they have a lot of worth, people of those castes do not get recognized. They are not lucky enough to be well

> *known. Many artists were buried in the depths of the past.*
> *There are no records that history has made a note of them*
> *in its pages. In this country, caste is more important than*
> *art. Art is also weighed on the scale of caste. As for those*
> *of certain castes, not just being weighed, they have not even*
> *been allowed near the scale. (ibid. p. 41)"*

Moreover, Kalyana Rao questions the sanctity of mainstream art and literature. He argues that though the songs have taken their birth in the labour of the down-trodden, their songs and literature are ignored, and they (the downtrodden) themselves have been alienated from the fruit of their labour.

The working castes engage in several productive tasks, which include 'ploughing the fields, making beds and watering them, plucking weeds; harvesting the crop, preparing the threshing floor; threshing and heaping the grain, separating the grains' etc. Despite their strenuous efforts in production, they do not possess the fields and grains as their property. They are estranged from the fruit of their toil. Karl Marx calls this social phenomenon the alienation of the working class, i.e., the producers alienation from production.

The labourers in villages weave and sing songs while carrying out their chores at the work spot. They take the themes for their songs from their daily life chores and produce great literature endowed with the imagery of pastoral lifestyle and beauty. There is no artificiality and hypocrisy in their literature as they weave songs quite naturally. In this context, Kalyana Rao voices against the narrow-minded mainstream scholars who do not acknowledge the literature of working castes. He raises the point hat if "Yenki – Nayudu Bava"songs represent Teluguness, the innumerable songs woven and sung by ordinary people in the fields should also represent Teluguness. Questioning the injustice done to the literature of the ordinary people, he brings several folklore characters such as Subbi, Koti, Lachchi, Maremma etc., to the notice of readers.

Another aspect of the art and literature of Dalits is that Dalits use and create literature as a revolt against the oppression and social injustice in society. They consciously revolt against oppression with their forms of art and literature, and this socio-revolutionary spirit can be found in the characters of Chandrappa, Naganna, Yellanna, and potter Peda Koteswarudu. Chandrappa, a great artist who knows the secrets of Puranas, tells them to young Naganna and makes him a great artist. Being well versed in several art forms such as Urumula dance, Bayalata of Rayalaseema, Veedhi Bagotam, he teaches Naganna various nuances of art and trains him up in Urumula dance. Chandrappa, who has natural anger towards the Brahmanic scholars, narrates many stories. While narrating Surasura Puranam, he lays bare the treachery of Brahmanic gods. B. Krylov writes,

> "*Marx and Engels revealed the social nature of art and its development in the course of history and showed that in a society with class antagonisms, it was influenced by class contradictions and by the politics and ideologies of particular classes. (Marx, Engels, On Literature, Progress Pub., Moscow, 1978, P. 17)*"

Similarly, we find in Chandrappa an ideological contradiction with the mainstream Brahmanic epics. The author shows this contradiction through the narration of a Dalit puranic tale by Chandrappa, who tells this story to Naganna, who in turn tells this to Yellanna. According to this puranic tale, Brahma, who is considered the creator of the universe, is a 'crook' as He did a huge injustice to Rakshasas [the aboriginal people of India] standing in support of gods [the Aryans who immigrated from Europe]. The children of Ganga [mother of Rakshasas] make Brahma and his rishis [the godmen and pundits] run around the 'three worlds'. The rishis who were chased by Ganga's children conspire and put on curtains for the play. They build tents around the curtains. Closing the temple doors, they performed Surasura Puranam. This tale reflects the antagonistic contradiction between two [the Aryan and the Dravidian] major cultural streams in India. While narrating this tale to Yellanna, Naganna comments sarcastically that the pundits cannot perform before people while Dalits can. He also proudly announces that it is not Bhagiratha [a rishi in Hindu mythology] who brought Ganga to the earth, but the urumula people. This story of Chandrappa is a justifiable expression of revolt against the oppressive mainstream art and literature.

The Art of Dalits - Street Plays

Street plays are part and parcel of Dalits' lives. Yellanna and the other members, being trained by Naganna, enact their play in front of people without dais and curtains. The language of the play is purely colloquial, and the theme and narration of the puranic tale are closely connected with the lives of ordinary people. The first performance is held at the malapalli of Yennela Dinni. People from the neighbouring mala and madiga palles come. Kalyana Rao here gives further evidence for such kinds of plays which were performed in several Telugu speaking regions. He writes that Sindhu Bagotam of the madigas in Telangana and Veedi Bagotam of the madigas in coastal Rayalaseema was widely known in those days.

It is an amazing experience for malas and madigas as they earlier used to watch the plays organized by village elders and upper castes from far. Now, they watch the play of Yellanna from close quarters and moreover, they do not fear whether the Karanam or some other elders would see as the performance is theirs and those who perform and those who watch are they themselves. Considering the unjust and vainglorious orders of the upper caste landlords are a blow to their self–respect, Naganna and Yellanna decide to abandon their performances. Yellanna's contemplation of this issue helps him transform himself into a song weaver, and thereby he becomes popular as 'Mala Bairagi'.

The Art of Song Weaving in the Down-Trodden Class

The art of song-weaving has been with the working castes for generations. They weave songs from the incidents which have taken place in the past or recent past. This historical reality is reflected in this novel. Varavara Rao writes,

"Brahmanism in India treats Dalits as untouchables. It is imposing untouchability on 'Spring'. The depressed castes, protesting this oppressive ideology, have long been fighting for ages. They are creating artistic struggles. In fact, as they know the aspects like searching for food and struggling for production, they know how to create an aesthetic world. Only the race which takes part in production does have culture. In this backdrop, Kalyana Rao depicts the struggles and literature of Dalits in the Coastal Andhra and Rayalaseema regions. (Bhoomitho matlaadu, Fiction and Content Analysis, Yuga Publications, 2005, print. p. 122)"

As Yellanna belongs to the class which engages itself in the struggle for production, he weaves songs naturally, taking the themes from the daily lives of Dalits. Kalyana Rao lays bare the hypocrisy of Brahmanist scholars who escape from recognizing the literature of the downtrodden. He explains how injustice was done to the writings of the writers like Potter Pedakoteswarudu and Yellanna by brahmin pundits in the days when Brown searched for Vemana's and others' writings.

Kalyana Rao further discusses the genuine efforts of Brown, a broad-minded English officer who did not have the opportunity to see the people like Yellanna. As he entirely depended on the Brahmin pundits, they would go around the villages and collect works; all satakas [one sataka means a volume of a hundred poems], all ancient Puranas (epics) and histories, Kasi Puranas, Vishnu Puranas, Surya Tanya Parinayam etc., were collected. Kalyana Rao criticizes the gluttony of scholars of the day. "Leaving aside Vemana, Kavi Chowdappa, Sumati Satakam, and Bhagavatam, they passed off even those that were not Telugu as Telugu. The Velagapudis, the Mulagapakas, the Ravipatis, the Chilakamarris, the Samudralas, the Tippabhatlus, the

Puranams, the Puvvadas - all of them together saw to it that there was no opportunity for the real Telugu word to be unearthed and to be preserved" (ibid. p. 97).

Kalyana Rao says that artists like Yellanna take the 'life out of people's culture'. However, as the author puts it, the Brahmin pundits, being opportunistic, give authority to the culture which is not of the people. Having an excessive zeal for retaining the power of their position, these scholars "do not hesitate to curry any kind of flavour". They force down the art and literature of a few people on the heads of the majority of the people. Glorifying the downtrodden art and literature, he criticizes the Brahmanist narrow–minded outlook. Kalyana Rao writes, "The art, the literature and the culture outside the temple became those of the ordinary people. All the lifeless struggles inside the temple became art and came to the fore. Shakuntala of Kalidasa and Varudhini of Allasani of the past, the recent Yenki of Nanduri and the present Kinnera of Viswanatha are all imagined beauties. But Yellanna's Subhadra is no figment of his imagination."(p. 98)

The literature that depicted the lives of "untouchables"is ignored by mainstream artists and writers. Because of this, the attempts to write the literature of the depressed have never been undertaken. In this context, we can find a similarity between Kalyana Rao's perception and Dr.B.R. Ambedkar's opinion. According to Dr B.R. Ambedkar: In every country, the intellectual class is the most influential class. This is the class that can foresee, advise and lead. In no country does the mass of the people live the life for intelligent thought and action. It is largely imitative and follows the intellectual class. There is no exaggeration in saying that the entire destination of the country depends upon its intellectual class. If the intellectual class is honest and independent, it can be trusted to take the initiative and give a proper lead when a crisis arises. It is true that the intellect by itself is no virtue. It is only a means, and the use of a means depends upon the ends which an intellectual person pursues. An intellectual man can be a good man, but he may easily be a rogue. Similarly, an intellectual class may be a band of high-souled persons, ready to help, ready to emancipate erring humanity, or it may easily be a gang of crooks or a body of advocates of narrow clique from which it draws its support. (google search)

We can infer from the way the character of Yellanna is treated that G. Kalyana Rao epitomized Yellanna as a proletarian folklorist paying tributes to the innumerable anonymous artists of the downtrodden through this character.

Potter Pedakoteswarudu's Dvipadas [couplets]

Potter Pedakoteswarudu writes dvipada [couplet] poems alongside making pots. The pundits, out of jealousy, comment that Koteswarudu's pots are better than his dvipdas and thereby 'lighten their heart's burden'. Kalyana Rao explains the vainglory of Brahmin pundits in this context. He reveals how the Brahmin pundits look down on the scholarship of the downtrodden. The author further says, the Brahmin pundits who alleged Brown as the enemy of Hinduism prostrated before him when he showed interest in dvipadas as the collection of dvipadas facilitated them to earn money. Also, they who criticized dvipadas as 'vidhavalanjalu' [Widow- prostitutes] worked as coolies at so many dvipadas a rupee when Brown showed interest in the dvipadas.

Pedakoteswarudu writes about Potuluri Veerabrahmam, who advocated social equality in society in his dvipadas. He gives up his caste and believes that everything is mud; all the people, regardless of their caste, are mud. Writing with this world outlook, he mingles with the lowest of the lowly. He eats and drinks at the houses of malas and madigas. Ignorant of the fact that Basavadu, a great social reformer and champion of the ordinary people, lived in the 12 th century A.D., he searches for him in vain. He continues his search for him till the end of his life.

As he meets 'mala bairagi', he is about to be attacked inexcusably by the vainglorious upper caste people who a Brahmin pundit instigated. On reaching the place where mala bairagi stays, he writes the songs of mala bairagi while they are being sung by mala bairagi himself. Miserably, after a few minutes of his departure, Pedakoteswarudu is killed by the upper caste people who chased him a few hours ago. The papers in which Pedakoteswarudu wrote the songs of mala bairagi are blood- stained, and later they are burnt away by the caste chauvinists. Mala bairagi and Ramanaiah complete the funeral rites of Pedakoteswarudu. Ramanaiah plants a sampenga sapling on his tomb and plants a fence of gangiregu trees around it. Thereafter, the tomb of potter Pedakoteswarudu has become a meeting place for the down-trodden. It is a fact that the lower caste intellectuals had often been killed by the upper caste people in the erstwhile feudal societies. This aspect is reflected in this novel through the characters of Pedakoteswarudu and Martin.

While Pedakoteswarudu writes dwipadas, Yellanna weaves songs. Roaming from village to village, he sings his songs which are even sung by the coolies while they work in the fields. The noticeable feature in his songs is the refrain 'Listen Subhadra' that his wife Subhadra also listens to when some coolies sing. The song is as follows:

Listen Subhadra.
The mouse drank the water under the roof. || Listen ||
Listen Subhadra.
How will it rain at a cloudless place? || Listen ||
Listen Subhadra.
How will the stream fill up without rain? || Listen ||
   Listen Subhadra.
How will the field become wet without stream filling? || Listen ||
Listen Subhadra.
How will we plant saplings without the field getting wet? || Listen ||
Listen Subhadra.
How will the cornflower without planting the saplings? || Listen ||
Listen Subhadra.
How will the grains fall without threshing the yield? || Listen ||
Listen Subhadra.
How will the granary fill without the grain falling? || Listen ||
Listen Subhadra.
How to pay back the namu without the granary filling? || Listen ||
Listen Subhadra.

The namu is paid back, hunger remains.
Listen Subhadra.
The mouse drank the water under the roof. || Listen || (p. 121- 122)

The entire song reflects the life of struggle of the masses. They endeavour day and night only to earn two meals a day. This very social reality is reflected in terms of clouds, rain, stream, plants, corn, grain, namu [grain loan], hunger etc. This song is a specimen that mirrors the poor lives of Dalits.

Transformation of Folk Songs to Progressive Songs

Kalyana Rao shows how folk songs get transformed into progressive or revolutionary songs with new words and meanings. After returning from work every day, the village folk eat food at night and go to the centre of the village where they have a lot of 'fun and frolic during the moonlit days'. They play Kolatam and learn new songs with old and new tunes. The words and meanings of the old song are as follows:

Tamarind tree flared, tamarind tree flared
what happened to the beams, it's deceit, Raja
I am young for sport.
I am young, I'm deceived, Raja
I'm young for sport. (ibid. p. 208)

This old song is changed to an entirely new song:
Why worries for us, why worries for us –
The hammer and sickle have come,
Move along, coolie! (ibid. p. 208)
'Tamarind tree flared' is, in fact, chintallu chelarege' in the Telugu version. The word 'chinta' has a double meaning. One is the 'tamarind tree', and the other is 'worry'. That is why the line "Tamarind tree flared "has become. "why worries for us."This change takes place in the literature of people because of the presence of the communist party in the village.

Struggle for Land

Land and water are the basis for all life that including social life. However,these resources are in the captivation of a few dominant people. The majority of thepeople who depend on agriculture have long been leading lives in poverty andadversity. They cultivate the land, but they do not have a small tenement of land. Hardships of life compel these masses to acquire at least a small piece of l and. They are compelled to acquire land either by pleas or by occupying empty lands that belong to the landlords or the government. This novel has reflected this socio-economic reality in the contexts of mala's mound in Yennela Dinni and Valasapadu land dispute episodes.

Kalyana Rao brings before us the illegal possession of lands by the dominant in this context. This novel discusses how the gifted lands that should lawfully belong to the artisans used to be in the captivation of the village administrators in pre- independent India. Being cultivated by none, mala's mound in Yennela Dinni is left vacant. In fact, several other fields do not count in the surroundings of Yennela Dinni. People know that those fields belong to karanam, but they do not see that they are all gifted lands. The people who belong to the washermen, barbers, potters, blacksmiths and carpenter castes do not know how much of the land is encroached upon by the karanam. People know that there are only two acres of land for potters' clay, but it is approximately five acres. The karanam encroached on the three acres of land. Similarly, the lake and six acres adjacent to it are in possession of washermen, but Karanam grabs the remaining tenements of land. Twenty-five acres are accounted for in the name of devadasis in that village, but he enjoys it in the name of god or devadasis' land. The gift of land in exchange for the bonded labour is cancelled with the grain measured out during harvest time. However, the bonded labourers cannot ask how much land they actually have. Even if they ask, karanam will not answer. The people of Yennela Dinni do not know that there is 'land gifted in exchange of work' because "those gifts are there in the karanam's accounts".

Acquisition of Mala's Mound

Kalyana Rao skillfully exposes the internal conflicts and contradictions among the ruling classes in this context. Besides Naganna's initiative, Atchireddy's enhanced dominance and younger karanam's envy and embarrassment help Dalits in Yennela Dinni acquire the malas' mound land. The essence of the unorganized struggles of the marginalized that often took place in history to acquire a small chunk of cultivable land for livelihood is reflected in this episode.

The landlessness and acute poverty compel Dalits in Yenneladinni to occupy mala's mound, an abandoned land densely covered with bushes, among which the elder karanam was assassinated by Mathaiah. Dalits, under the leadership of Naganna, have no intention of occupying the malas' mound, which is also known as devil's mound, violently. When they cut half of the trees, it attracts villagers attention, and therefore the village elders summon them to be present under the 'geviti' [Neem] tree in the morning. The younger karanam and Atchireddy sit on the platform under the geviti tree, but Atchireddy's occupation of the seat just beside him makes the younger karanam feel pretty unpleasant. Naganna explains that his people have thought of cleaning it up as mala's mound has remained unused. It is noticed by the younger karanam that there is amity and unity between malas and madigas who used to complain against them even about trivial reasons sitting in separate groups. Naganna says they came to know that he [the younger karanam] had gone to Nellore when they wanted to convey this matter beforehand.

Younger karanam's ego is satiated at the words of Naganna as he thinks that those words are appropriate to his status. He has observed for some days that Bukkireddy is occupying his father's [Elder karanm's] place, while Atchireddy recently emerges as a landlord by annexing some wastelands to his fields. Under all these circumstances, the younger karanam gives mala's mound to malas and madigas. The author reveals in this context that the basis for either unity or disunity is property (production) relations and the nature of which is determined by political power.

The mala's mound, at last, comes into cultivation. The malas and madigas distribute the land among themselves. The author reminds the readers about the sacrifice and courage of Narigadu and Mataiah. Kalyana Rao writes that the sacrifice of Narigadu and Mataiah helped them achieve mala's mound. He further says in this connection that the struggle is not an ideal for Dalits but a "necessity"as without the struggle, they can never attain equality and justice. The author is often found to intervene in the middle of the story and voices against the social injustice to which Dalits have unjustly been subjected by the dominant. He says:

> "*Struggle is not an ideal for malas and madigas. It is a necessity. There is no page in the history of the struggle of this country that has not been soaked in their blood. There is no instance which is not connected with their courage. They have fought for their self-respect. The present too is the same. The present life struggle, too, is the same. That is not an ideal. A necessity. (ibid. p. 87- 88)*"

It is, of course, under certain dramatic conditions the malas and madigas attain land without bloodshed in the novel, but on most of the occasions, the landlords and the dominant never allow the oppressed to get lands through peaceful agitations. There are numerous instances of this in history. The author depicts such an incident --the Valasapadu Land issue-- in chapter 14. It lays bare the oppressive nature of the dominant castes.

Valasapadu Land Issue

Dalits who have been cast away from the fourfold caste system are subjected to physical and mental harassment by the upper caste landlords whenever they embrace Christianity, free from the caste system. While they are converted to Christianity, they are unjustifiably imprisoned and tortured. Varavara Rao writes:

"Dalits, who converted to Christianity to achieve equal social status, were attacked by upper castes in the Guntur district. As Christianity became the religion of the ruling class in British India, the upper castes too became Christians. Thus, not only the untouchability in Hinduism but also the land-related struggles in Hindu feudalism continued without undergoing any change. (Bhoomitho matlaadu, Fiction and Content Analysis, Yuga Publications, 2005, p. 120)"

This social reality is reflected in the scenes of Martin's murder and the devastation of Valasapadu village. In Valasapadu village, Dalits, subjected to social eviction by the caste Hindus, cannot find work for their livelihood. When they think of returning to their native places, they happen to find twenty-five acres of barren land fallen vacant. Their struggle for land begins with Martin's plea to the authorities to give away the barren land to the poor Christians, also Dalits. Here, spontaneously we remember the words of Frederic Engels [one of the proponents of scientific socialism], who says that the struggles organized by the followers of Christ were also of the proletarian in essence during the beginning centuries after the crucifixion of Christ. Because Martin's selfless efforts to fetch a smaller tenement of land remind us about the socio- spiritual practice of the followers of Christ even after the crucifixion of Christ. They, too, fought to support the downtrodden until Christianity was declared the 'state – religion' by the Byzantine emperor around 330 A.D. On the advice of the authorities, when Martin meets them again after a week, they tell him that the land is not barren land. He meets the village karanam, who says that the land is owned by two farmers. Later Martin meets the British officer requesting him to do justice. Meanwhile, a rumour spread that Christians are grabbing the properties of farmers. The upper–caste people file a case in the court.

Immanuel Sastry, the son-in-law of the younger karanam of Yennela Dinni, argues for the upper castes. Martin meets and asks him to do justice to the poor Dalits, telling him two reasons: first, the land does not belong to anyone, and second, Immanual Sastry is a Christian, so he should stand for the poor fellow Christians. However, to the surprise of Martin, Immanual Sastry says that the other two farmers are also Christians who got baptized in Nellore just before the case comes to him. When Martin argues that the land should be given to the poor Dalit Christians, Immanuel Sastry callously says that all are Christians, whatever caste they belong to. As the author opines, even the upper castes too got converted to Christianity to acquire property and protect the same by endearing themselves to the British officers during the British regime. This historical reality is reflected in this context.

Martin understands the mind of Immanuel Sastry and finds dishonesty in his words. His conversation with Immanuel Sastry makes him tenacious in fighting against the dominant class. Finally, his efforts bear fruit when the land is proved to be barren and occupied by none. The 'white man' gives the right to cultivate the land to the poor Christians of that village. However, the decision of the authorities stokes up the anger of the upper castes who have felt defeated. Being unable to accept the verdict against their economic interests, they attack Martin, whom Simon then accompanied. They kill Martin and thrash and torture Simon, who later goes back home carrying the dead body of Martin and finds Sasirekha, Saramma and others remain dead. He understands that the upper caste people attacked the village and killed them. All this happens when the villagers are happy about getting the land and want to celebrate Christmas grandly. The violent attack on Martin takes place when they are returning to their village. The violent attacks on Dalits by the upper castes in society are reflected in this episode. Killing malas and madigas and torching their huts, the violent attack continues further on the village. The description of the violent attack on Valasapadu is as follows:

"*Holding the bloody body on his shoulders, the ghastly dance Simon saw. The scene of the graveyard of Valasapadu.*

> *The upper castes chasing the malas and madigas with spears and crowbars. The helpless running away in frenzy and fear. Their cries of agony. The constellation of ghosts that surrounded the palle. Did not know how many they killed. Did not know how many fled and in what direction. The thatched huts burning. The smoke from flames touched the sky. Saramma turned into a corpse. Simon gazing wide- eyed at those corpses and the flames surrounding them. (ibid. p. 176)"*

Even though Kalyana Rao does not explain the specific reasons for violence in the Valasapadu issue in this context, we can infer three causes for this bloodshed. Such ghastly incidents often occur with impunity in feudal and semi-feudal societies: First, the economic interests of the exploitative class. Second, when compared with upper castes, Dalits have only a subhuman status, so they have no right to raise their heads before the dominant people. However, in this context, they not only raise their heads but also defeat the upper castes in the court of law. Third, they embrace Christianity. Dalits, under the leadership of Martin, achieved the lands lawfully. In fact, the feudal lords could not tolerate the endeavours of the poor to become self- reliant. If the poor become self-reliant, the landlords cannot get cheap labour to get their lands cultivated and thereby, they themselves shall have to work in the fields, shedding sweat. This cannot be imagined and invited by any landlord. That is why the landlords often resort to unleashing violence on the downtrodden with impunity whenever they go against their vested interests.

Floods and Droughts: The Miseries of Dalits

The depressed castes are the major victims of floods and droughts. Though Dalits in Yennela Dinni live on the threshold of danger, they have no other way to live in safety. They are ordered to live at the feet of the upper caste both socially and geographically.

That is why, when the malas and madigas think of building their houses on the mound, the vacant upland of the village, the upper castes do not consider their justified need. However, unfair social restrictions are sometimes ruled out by the victims. People ignore such unjustifiable social restrictions when they are entangled between the devil and the deep sea. This social reality is reflected in this context. The malas and madigas of Yennela Dinni also do the same when Narigadu decides to move to the mound during that ferocious night. When the others are reluctant to move, Narigadu dares to go. The courage of Narigadu inspires madiga Mataiah and later all other people. They made up their minds to save their lives from floods. However, the age-old inhuman customs make them hesitate to reach the mound passing through the streets of the upper castes who have, until then, prohibited the entry of Dalits into their streets. The fear of death and innate desire to be alive prompt them to reach the mala's mound through the upper castes streets.

There, the malas and the madigas cook and eat together. The author comments that the floods have brought them together. In this context, the author shows the unity that emerged spontaneously between the two castes--malas and madigas-- in Dalits, but why the disunity that has long been existing between them is left untouched. While the floods have brought them together, what had separated them earlier is also a worth considering question that should have been discussed. The author, in this regard, seemed to have deliberately avoided the discussion of Brahmanism that has crept even in the castes of Dalits. Quite miserably, the hierarchical structure, based on birth and social status, is found even in Dalits. All the castes in Dalits do not enjoy the same equal social status. This is a specimen of the fact that Brahmanism badly influenced every section of people in this country. This is why B.R. Ambedkar exhorts that it is Brahmanism, not the Brahmin individuals, to be eliminated.

How hunger provokes a man to steal things to fill his belly is realistically depicted in this context. The next day, when they have nothing to eat, Narigadu and Mataiah steal rice from the 'sahukar's shop'. Besides their settlement on the mound, stealing provisions from the shop of an upper caste person adds fuel to the fire in the village elders who murder Narigadu. A violent agitation by the oppressed that rarely take place in society is reflected in this episode. Mataiah takes vengeance for the cruel murder of Narigadu. He kills elder karanam with Narigadu's axe. The villagers talk among themselves that some ghost has killed the elder karanam. After that, the mound comes to be known as devils mound or mala's mound. The vengeance of Mataiah mirrors the violent agitation that is occasionally embraced by the oppressed in the uneven and unjustifiable society.

The Lives of the Downtrodden during the Drought

While the ordinary caste Hindus suffer from poverty, the untouchables suffer from both poverty and untouchability. The intensity of these sufferings is enormous during the period of drought. G. Kalyana Rao heartrendingly depicts the miserable conditions of Dalits during a famine in this novel. The 'Datu' drought and the living conditions of people and especially those of Dalits during this drought are reflected in this episode. Suravaram Pratap Reddy writes:

> *"This Datu drought occurred in 1876 -1878 in the then Indian provinces: Bombay [now Mumbai] and Madras [now Chennai]. Besides other regions, the Telugu speaking regions were severely affected by this famine. During this famine, lakhs of Telugu people died of starvation. According to English historians, about fifty lakhs of people lost their lives only in the Deccan region (the then Hyderabad State). (cited from Akkiraju Ramapathi Rao's article "Telugunata Karuvu Vishadalu" published in Andhrajyothi, The Daily Newspaper, 13 Dec 2015, print.)"*

Because of the severe drought known as Datu drought and famine, lakhs of people died of starvation and cholera in Southern India regardless of their socioeconomic status. The grave consequences of the Datu famine are heartrendingly reflected in this novel. Even landlords like Atchireddy and Chukkireddy are unable to withstand the drought and die. While the conditions of the poorer reddys are bad, the conditions of the malas and madigas are worse than all other castes in Yennela Dinni. The description of 'Datu Karuvu' in the novel is as follows:

> "*The severe drought known as Datu Karuvu took the lives of lakhs of people in southern India. No rains. No crops. No work, nothing at all on the parched earth. People ate leaves. They ate weeds ... The bonta fruit did not help them survive. Nagajemudu began to create burning in the stomach. They drank muddy water, thinking it would infuse life. Even so, hunger deaths did not stop; they died violently, shaking their legs. They died straining their stomachs. They died contracting diarrhoea. They went on starving and dying. Along with it, cholera.(ibid. p. 129)*"

The people in the surrounding villages begin to move in groups in search of employment where the Buckingham canal works are being carried out. Yellanna, who understands that he is in his last days, decides to return to Yennela Dinni. On his way back to his village, he visits the tomb of Peddakoteswarudu. However, there are no sampenga flowers on the tomb. It has become half dry and struggles for life. It symbolizes the critical condition of Yellanna, who is also in his last days. He has become half-dead and begun to struggle to be alive, at least until he reaches Yennela Dinni. He does not find Ramanaiah over there, and so he does not feel like staying there. Weaving songs within himself, he resumes his journey to Yennela Dinni.

Death has taken a heavy toll on all, regardless of their castes. From the wealthy landlords like Atchireddy to the downtrodden people like Pittodu, Chinnammi, Boodevi, Yenkatanarsu, and several others die of starvation in Yennela Dinni. It is Sivaiah who digs the pits and buries the dead bodies of his people. In this context, Kalyana Rao reminds us about the intensity of the man-woman relationship. The author shows this through the characters of Yellanna and Subhadra. At every pit, Subhadra sits like a 'haunted spirit'. She still waits for her Yellanna as her deepest aspiration to see her consort again--at least once-- makes her alive.

Hoping to get at least one palmyra fruit, Sivaiah digs in vain a large and deep pit that is big enough for two persons to be buried. Being in panic at such a thought, he throws the spade right there and goes out of the village. He sees several migrants who 'holding their hunger in their stomachs' are on their way to the Buckingham canal for digging work. Amid the crowd, he happens to see a staggering man who is about to die soon and utters only one word, 'Subhadra'. Getting startled at the incoherent lisping of Yellanna, he thinks that the man may be his father, so he carries him to his house, where Subhadra identifies him as her Yellanna. She hugs him to her heart. Yellanna breathes his last in the lap of his beloved, and Subhadra too dies holding her husband. Just as she had aspired, she was alive until she met her husband. In this context, the author G. Kalyana Rao with his heart touching depiction, duly extols the intimacy in the man-woman relationship:

> "*Subhadra ... Subhadra, Only that word. Father and son. Mother and daughter. What was this bond? Whatever there was, was only one bond. It could be for the haves. Could also be for the have – nots. Could be for the upper castes. Could be for the untouchables. Only one eternal bond. The husband–and–wife bond. ' I and my Subhadra. She and I'. He was unable to say all these words aloud. Was able to say just one word. Subhadra ... Subhadra. (ibid. p. 133)*"

Yellanna and Subhadra, who were alive until their communion die together, clasping each other. Sivaiah dislikes separating them, so he buries them together in the pit dug for a tender palmyra sprout. "Beneath the mud, the song and the pallavi. On top of it, their echoes". Having decided to migrate somewhere for livelihood, he and his wife Sasirekha mingle with migrants. Several of them die on the way. The remaining people do not have the energy to bury their bodies. Sivaiah and Sasirekha continue their journey with great hope. On their way, they come across a young boy and a girl. His name is Jinkodu, and the girl is his friend. It can be inferred that to reveal the quickly built intimate relationships among the downtrodden, that is not the property owned class, Kalyana Rao has created Jinkodu and his girlfriend characters in this episode.

Walking as it becomes dark, they halt at a mango grove and find water, but they do not know whether it is good. As they have no other option, they drink it and later on, they 'rest their backs on the sand'. When Sasirekha and the girl fall asleep, Jinkodu proposes to Sivaiah that both of them could go to the village nearby and try whether they could get any food. They go to a village and enter a house wherein they find a half-eaten food plate. Hearing the words, ' my husband ... died without eating all of it', Sivaiah and Jinkodu get startled and look in the direction from which those words come. An older woman speaks those words sitting beside a dead body of an older man. When Jinkodu takes the plate of food into his hand, the older woman unexpectedly attacks and chases them, but she becomes prey for the hungry stray dogs. Sivaiah is unable to take his share of food while Jinkodu and the girl eat it. However, the girl died that night due to diarrhoea. On hearing the loud crying of Jinkodu, Sivaiah and Sasirekha wake up. Saying he would join them later if possible, Jinkodu asks them to resume their journey.

On reaching the place where the digging work of the Buckingham canal is being carried out, Sivaiah gets perplexed, unable to understand whom he should approach. He finds at a distance a 'rotund man' who looks strange. Though he does not state specifically that the rotund man is an upper caste chauvinist, he intends to give an idea to his readers by describing the appearance and attitude of the rotund man. "The man looked strange. The way he wore his pancha [a garment that covers a man's body from waist to feet] was strange. Sivaiah found waring a pancha on a shirt something new. He had a leather belt over it. On his forehead were three well-drawn vertical lines" (ibid. p. 140).

When Sivaiah tells his identity that he is a mala from Yennela Dinni, the rotund man starts to 'scream like an insane man'. In his opinion, the malas and madigas have no right to work equally on par with the upper castes. Miserably, the poor caste people who are working there as coolies too believe in the same ideology and join hands with the upper caste people in attacking Sivaiah and Sasirekha. Kalyana Rao depicts this social injustice realistically in this context.

Socio - Economic Problems: Religious Conversions

While Sivaiah and Sasirekha become Christians to save their lives from hunger, Chinnodu alias Martin and Polamma alias Saramma embrace Christianity to live with self–respect. In addition to Dalits, people from the upper castes become Christians only to befriend the English officers and thereby become wealthy and
protect their unlawfully acquired property. While the pathetic living conditions cause Dalits to become Christian converts, the greed for wealth makes the upper caste people embrace Christianity. This social scenario is reflected in this novel.

Chinnodu and Polamma

By narrating the trials and tribulations of Chinnodu and Polamma, the author tries to give an account of the pathetic living conditions of Dalits who are often subject to exploitation, privation, humiliations at the hands of upper-caste landlords and how the poverty originated from the contemporary exploitative production system, causes trivial disputes among the members of the poor. Chinnodu, who does not evince interest in pursuing his hereditary occupation of slipper stitching, despises the harassment of feudal lords in the village. He is vexed with the life he leads, and therefore he spends most of his time at the lake bund,
thinking of a solution to liberate himself from the humiliating living conditions. Also, he does not like his wife to go to Kapu's house for

work. Being unable to prevent his wife from going there, he gets angry with himself. Kalyana Rao implicitly tells us by describing the trauma of Chinnodu that some upper caste landlords and wealthy farmers often misbehave with the Dalit woman - coolies. The writer depicts the irritation of Chinnodu as:

"If she went for work to the kapu's house with her [co–sister], he would get inexplicably irritated. He would be angry with himself. He would not understand the reason for that irritation. There would be no concrete shape to his anger. He would not find an answer as to why he was so bitter with himself. ... How much irritation in those looks, how much anger, how much vengeance, and how much tears in the eyes when nothing was fulfilled? (ibid. p. 153)."

Another significant aspect in connection with Chinnodu's story is the production relations (property relations or social relations) that exist among the members of the families of the poor. Although family relations are primary relations, they too sustain on economic aspects on most occasions. Hence, the relations among the members of a family are also production relations. This social reality is reflected in the scene of a 'separate establishment' in Chinnodu's family. When the 'separate establishment' issue comes for discussion between Chinnodu and his brother, their father proposes that he stay with Chinnodu to take the job of stitching slippers in ten kapu houses for the grains he receives in return. As his father stitches slippers for fifteen houses, he too would get food grains from those houses. However, his sister- in-law vetoes the proposal arguing that the grains of all the fifteen houses should be hers, as father-in-law has been staying in her house. This leads to a squabble between the mother-in-law and the daughter-in-law. In this context, Kalyana Rao narrates how the labour of Dalits is exploited and how this exploitation makes the family members in the houses of Dalits quarrel with one another. He explains how the rich farmers deceive the indentured malas and madigas who get only half the amount of grains. The baskets which are used to measure grains are half the size of the normal ones. With this lesser quantity of grains, they are unable to lead lives and consequently, there are usually petty quarrels among the family members. Kalyana Rao expresses his annoyance in this context by comparing the Dalit workers with dumb beasts like 'oxen and cows'. Dalits, instead of fighting against exploitation, often resort to quarrelling with one another among themselves. We can understand the intent of the author if we look at the following paragraphs:

The malas and madigas never kept count of it. Had the bullock that had kept its neck under the yoke ever counted the acres that it had tilled? Did it ever count the number of hours the yoke rested on its neck? Had

the cow with its udder overflowing with milk been guilty of counting the number of pots of milk it gave on a particular day? When it seemed its calf came running and touched its udder, thinking it was its child, it filled the udder with milk, and when instead of the milk teeth at the udder, hands skillfully squeezed out the milk, did it ever get angry and kick? The cow and the bullock thought that a little grass and a tubful of kuditi was enough. Isn't kuditi but the water that was left behind after the kapus ate and washed their hands? Isn't the grass the dried one which was left after the seeds had dropped? That very kuditi and grass became the property to be divided in their house. Became the cause for displeasure. Became the cause for abuses. (ibid. p. 154 – 155)

Kalyana Rao is critical of the mean frailty of the Dalit youth who accept the debasing comments of the upper caste lords as compliments. The author expresses his disgust through the portrayal of the character of Yerrodu. Chinnodu hates to listen to the words of Yerrodu, who speaks about kapus and their abuses as if they were compliments. Yerrodu does not bother when he is addressed as a 'bastard', and they shamefully comment on his wife and mother. This hatred is not the hatred of the mere character but the hatred of the author himself. Being a Dalit, the author admonishes the vulgarity of the landlords and the weak-mindedness of fellow Dalits like Yerrodu. The author reveals his hatred of such human degradation through the fuming feelings of Chinnodu. "In whose bed did you conceive him?' those words would not affect Yerrodu. "... as he hears Yerrodu's words, he spits on the ground. He spits repeatedly. He thinks it is better to look at the spit than at Yerrodu's face. (ibid. p. 157)

How trials and tribulations cause the change in ideas and ideals is shownthrough the character of Chinnodu. The gradual change in Chinnodu, a docile manwho becomes a rebel until then, is depicted in a context. Chinnodu's inherent rebellious nature manifests itself when younger kapu comes over there. While everybody stands with folded hands as a token of respect, Chinnodu does not stand up. The younger kapu, who does not tolerate Chinnodu's adamant behaviour, thrashes him. Chinnodu is released and taken home by his mother and wife. Showing disobedience to the cruel and oppressive landlords is also a form of revolt. Kalyana Rao says:

> *"For Chinnodu's mother, it might be a blow on her womb. For Polamma, it might be a heart - wrenching blow. But for Chinnodu, it was a confrontation. A silent revolt against something he hated." (ibid. p. 158)*

A few days after this incident, Chinnodu's life takes an unexpected turn when a Christian missionary comes to his village. Chinnodu goes there and looks at the 'white man and white horse in amazement'. The white man holds his hand and affectionately places his hand on his shoulder. Until then, no caste Hindu has touched him, whereas now a white man has touched him. Chinnodu gets attracted towards the white man who has touched him, whom until then no upper-caste man has ever touched. When the white man says that Chinnodu's body is not untouchable, he keeps looking at the white man in admiration for a long time. Chinnodu, with his wife Polamma, moves along with the team of missionaries for one month. Later the white man baptizes Chinnodu and Polamma with water. As being baptized, Chinnodu gets excited, hoping that he too becomes as touchable as a brahmin or a reddy. When he asks the same, he is disappointed hearing the answer from the Whiteman. "Now, is this body like a brahmin's? Like a reddy's body? Can touch everything? Can touch everyone? ... But he did not give him a straightforward reply. ' For Christ, nobody is untouchable.' He only said those words. Chinnodu heard them. The answer was not straightforward. Was not clear." (ibid. p. 159)

The white man renames Chinnodu and Polamma as Martin and Saramma, respectively. However, Chinnodu turned Martin cannot get straight forward answer to his question. While the Manu code backed Hinduism do not let Dalits enter the caste Hindus' houses and their temples, the Christianity of the West has hugged affectionately and invited them to the places of worship and further, the Christian preachers and the British officers have allowed them into their houses and kitchens. In this regard, Christianity is progressive. As the people of upper castes also embraced Christianity, the practice of the caste system has intruded even in Christianity. This aspect of social reality is also reflected in this novel. Sivaiah becomes Simon Martin's pure heart and affectionate talk attract Sivaiah. It is Martin who protects Sivaiah and Sasirekha from the attacks of the upper caste people. Not that he gives them food and shelter, but it is the honesty of Martin that has attracted Sivaiah, who embraces Christianity and becomes Simon named after Simon in the Bible who carried the Cross along with Christ. The author evokes feelings of sympathy in readers minds by drawing similarities between Simon in the Holy Bible and Sivaiah. While Simon in the Bible carried the Cross along with Christ, Sivaiah, who became Simon, carried Martin's dead body, killed by the upper castes. The author, in this context, symbolically conveys that Dalits have long been carrying the Cross of social injustice.

Even after embracing Christianity, Dalits are not able to liberate themselves from the curse of untouchability. While Dalits embrace Christianity to protect their self-respect, the greedy rich upper caste people convert to Christianity to acquire wealth. These converts have retained Dalits in their traditionally imposed socio - economic chains.

The Upper Caste Converts

The son-in-law of the younger karanam of Yennela Dinni becomes Immanuel Sastry. Martin and Simon identify some other upper caste persons who have become Christians in the crowd. Even though they get converted to Christianity, they do not renounce their caste identity. That is why they are still willing to be called with their caste names, such as John Paul Reddy, Immanuel Sastry, Joshuah Choudary, etc. It is for the patronage of the British rulers that they have embraced Christianity in which both the oppressors and the oppressed are under the same umbrella. This causes mental turmoil in his mind, and this aspect makes him feel a sense of insecurity.

We can clearly understand the standpoint of the author through the words of Martin. The author opines that only Dalits are to be allowed into Christianity because when the upper caste people also embrace Christianity, they become upper-caste Christians and continue to practice untouchability in Christianity. The author reminds us about the ideas and efforts of a humane British Indian Christian, Clough, who lived

in India and did not agree to the upper caste conversions, forecasting the prospective caste discriminations that could inevitably creep into Christianity too. Kalyana Rao conveys this through the words of Martin, who says to Simon:

> "*Clough, the white man, did not accept this. His wife didn't accept. They mingled only with malas and madigas. They converted them to Christianity. The white man Clough's wife said it was Christ's decision to protect only the untouchables, Clough too believed that. He said he couldn't shut the gates to untouchables because of the upper—caste people. But everyone among whites is not like Clough. Not like Cotton. (ibid. p. 167)*"

Attacks on Dalit Christians

Having had subhuman status in Hinduism, Dalits are considered untouchables. When they get converted to Christianity, the upper caste Hindu chauvinists attack them. Sometimes, they imprison Dalits and torture them. This horrible social reality is reflected in this novel. The author Kalyna Rao opines that these are not the attacks on Christians as either the brahmins or reddys or other upper caste people who are converted to Christianity are never attacked. However, only Dalits are attacked, and the Bible in their hands is burnt. The basis for the contextual inclusion of the attacking scenes on Dalits is the real attacks that took place in Markapuram, Kanigiri, Bandlamoodi, and Cheemakurthi regions in the then Madras State [now Andhra Pradesh] a few years ago.

The author Kalyana Rao puts forth the atrocities conducted on the Dalit Christians in the areas mentioned above: Sixteen mala and madiga Christians were jailed in Markapuram and tortured there and forced to forget Christ and pray to Krishna in vain as they sang only Christian songs. The Bibles in their hands were
burnt. There was an attack on Christians in Bandlamoodi village at midnight. In Kuchipudi, the Dalit Christians were asked to dip themselves in the lake of the village and get rid of their Christian touch. They were forced to prostrate before the idol of Poleramma.

According to the feudal sanctions cruelly imposed by the upper castes in the then feudal societies, an untouchable should not walk in the village. Wearing slippers, he should walk past the upper caste people. He should not have a headcloth and hold an umbrella in his hand. He should not raise his lowered head. He should not look sideways, even accidentally. If an upper caste woman comes out and looks at him, he is subject to punishment. That is why Dalits are supposed to make a strange sound while walking in the village. Even if they make such a sound, if any upper-caste woman working somewhere in the backyard does not hear the sound and comes out, the fault will be his. There were such miserable living conditions in which Dalits led lives a few decades ago. In order to mirror all these maladies, Kalyana Rao depicts the cruel murder of a Dalit Christian in the same context.

One day, the upper castes hound and catch a madiga youth, charging him with two crimes. He has the Bible in his hand and wears slippers, so he has upset the tradition. That is why they chase him up to the outskirts of the village and stab him with spears, and hung his corpse from a tree in a little forest through which the malas and madigas go to the neighbouring villages. Describing the plight of Dalits, Kalyana Rao comments on how Dalits are suppressed and oppressed in every sphere of social life:

> "*Some malas and madigas wore clean clothes. There was an attack on those clothes. ... They were attacked for expressing their views on 'eating' such things. They started to study a little bit in missionary schools. There was an attack on that education. Here and there, the untouchables raised their heads and looked. There was an attack on their heads. ... Attack on the mala people. On the madiga people. Attack. On the mala Christ. Attack on the madiga Christ. It would be enough if Christ were untouchable. (ibid. p. 170)*"

Lorose
Struggle for Access to the Public Utilities

G. Kalyana Rao rebukes the inhuman practice of the deprivation of Dalits from access to public utilities. Temple entry and lake water dispute episodes mirror this social injustice that Dalits have been subject to for generations together. He mocks at the insincere and selfish attempts of the landlords, who are the leading part of Harijan Sevak Sangh that was formed with the 'blessings' of Gandhiji.

Harijan Sevak Sangh

The writer G. Kalyana Rao pinpoints the hypocrisy of Harijan Sevak Sangh workers. With the aim of wiping out the stain on Hinduism, the Harijan Sevak Sangh was formed on 11 December 1932. The main objective of this organization is to work for the well being of the 'untouchables' whom Gandhiji called Harijans,

the children of God. Gandhiji's conception is that "the Harijans are creditors and the caste Hindus
who introduced the sin of untouchability are debtors, and therefore, it is the duty of the debtors to work for the removal of untouchability and the upliftment of the Harijans". The duties of the workers of Harijan Seva Sangh include: Every social worker should have a zeal to purify Hinduism and should be ready to sacrifice his 'family connections and social advantages' for this noble social cause. Furthermore, the workers of Harijan Seva Sangh are to strive for achieving equal rights for the untouchables over the utilization of public wells, roads, temples etc.

However, in reality, the Harijan Seva Sanghs become a mere platform for the development of the political career of the landlords like Linga Reddy. The author opines that the untouchables cannot achieve social justice through the insincere efforts of such organizations. In fact, the usage of the term 'Harijan' itself is not acceptable to the author. He severely condemns the usage of this term through the conversation between Reuben and Ramanujam. When Reuben asks about his opinion on using the word 'Harijan' by Gandhiji, Ramanujam says the word Harijan in no way is better than mala and madiga. Ramanujam further states that while the Brahminical society makes malas and madigas untouchables, Gandhiji, with the word Harijan, makes them 'orphans' as well.

G. Kalyana Rao reveals the nexus between the landlords and Gandhiji through the character of Lingareddy. He also ridicules the dual nature of the landlords who maintain good relations with both the political parties --Congress Party and the Justice Party-- which are opposite to each other. Linga Reddy is the disciple of Gandhiji and the leader of Harijan Seva Sangh work. It is due to his good relations with the British authorities of the region that he can increase his land, and at the same time, because of his association with Gandhiji, he becomes a patriot too. In order to gain the support of Ramanujam, who is a communist, Linga Reddy tries to befriend him also. Now he takes the responsibility of Harijan Seva Sangh of Nellore district.

The Activities of Harijan Seva Sangh Workers

On gathering in a village, the workers of Harijan Seva Sangh give slogans 'Jai to Gandhiji'. Afterwards, singing patriotic songs, they begin to sweep the streets of Dalits. Linga Reddy himself takes part in the cleaning activity to the surprise of Dalits. After sweeping the streets, the drinking of water in the houses of the untouchables is scheduled. This episode takes place in a highly 'exaggerated' manner. They keep a giant cauldron for collecting water from the houses of untouchables, and each house has to pour a pot of water while the workers sing songs and make speeches in which they reiterate that untouchability is a crime. The lectures last for nearly an hour near the cauldron, followed by drinking water by all. With the raising of the slogan 'Jai to Gandhi', the programme for that day is concluded. When Ramanujam comes over there at the end of the programme, Linga Reddy hugs him and asks him to participate in the temple entry programme scheduled the next day.

Temple Entry

The temple entry programme of Harijan Seva Sangh is proved deceitful in this episode. In fact, the writer opines that this temple entry programme aims to protect the Hindu religion from mass conversions rather than eradicate untouchability in society. This novel reflects the superficiality of the temple entry programmes organized by Harizan Seva Sanghs in those days. As part of the so-called reformative programme, the workers of Harijan Seva Sangh selected the temples located outside the village and invited Dalits to enter them. These programmes were proved to be ineffective in bringing in any progressive change in the social status of Dalits. Because their houses were located outside the village and the temples they were allowed to enter also were located outside the village. However, the workers of Harijan Seva Sangh never dared to act against the conservative civil society, though they took an oath that they would sacrifice their 'family connections and social advantages' for the noble social cause. Even if Dalits were allowed to enter the temples in the village, there used to be purificatory rituals afterwards. This social reality is reflected in this episode.

After renovating the Siva temple outside the village, the Seva Sangh workers come with great pomp on the day of the temple entry. The elders of the village invite the village folk to join the procession while the workers sing songs about the temple entry of Harijans. After making speeches by workers, the procession starts in which Ramanujam too takes part. Lingareddy expresses happiness as Ramanujam, too, has attended the programme. When the procession is about to go past the village to reach the Siva temple outside, Ramanujam asks that the procession proceeds into the village. Ramanujam demands that the temple entry programme be held at Vishnu or Rama temple in the village itself. The Seva Sangh workers try to dissuade Ramanujam from giving up his demand in vain. This demand is soon transformed into an argument between Ramanujam and Harijan Seva Sangh workers. Standing in support of Ramanujam's proposal, the youngsters warn the elders that they withdraw from the programme. Being unable to do anything, Lingareddy orders that the procession should go into the village. When the procession enters the compound of the Temple, Linga Reddy cleverly draws Ramanujam into an argument to divert his attention. Meanwhile, the priest comes out along with harathi. The people who push and shove among themselves in a frenzy to receive harathi forget to fulfil their demand of the entry of sanctum sanctorum. It is not known to them that they were deceived by having been prevented from entering the temple sanctum sanctorum. That night, Lingareddy gets the "temple compound and steps purified with cow dung and cow's urine as priests recite mantras". G. Kalyana Rao sarcastically comments on this purificatory ritual. He says:

> "*As idealistically as they performed the societal service called temple entry of Harijans, they also did the purificatory task of the temple in a similarly pious manner. In fact, there was such flexibility in Gandhij's mode. If that were not so, Gandhiji would not have appeared so great to people like Lingareddy. (ibid. p. 200)*"

While Lingareddy is getting the purificatory task done, Venkatadri, a Dalit Harijan Sevak Sangh worker too is present there along with other workers. Lingareddy does not know that Venkatadri is also a 'Harijan' who cannot digest the purificatory ritual at the temple. He feels betrayed by the village elders. He meets Ramanujam and tells him about the betrayal of Lingareddy. Ramanujam says that the programme of the upliftment of Harijans is being done to bind the malas and madigas in the Hindu religious frame. Venkatadri, along with Ramanujam, Reuben and Ruth, reaches Bitragunta railway station to complain against Lingareddy. However, He finds the landlord Lingareddy amid the important people waiting for Gandhi to welcome him. Shivering with anger, he says that he would show the actual form of Lingareddy to the Nellore reddys and when he is about to go in front, Ramanujam dissuades him from his attempt. Meanwhile, the Calcutta mail in which Gandhiji is travelling arrives at the station. Gandhiji leaves for Kavali by car, and Venkatadri is disillusioned.

G. Kalyana Rao ridicules the untouchability eradication programme of Gandhiji through the discussion between the characters of Ramanujam and Reuben. In this context discussing the rules of 'Agama Satra', the author contrasts the ideologies of Gandhiji and Periyar on the caste system. Though Gandhiji declares that there is no sanctity for untouchability in the Vedas, Puranas and the other Hindu sastras, he often says that Harijans would have the right to enter temples only when they follow the principles of 'Agama Sastram'. Ramanujam says that those who support the caste system argue that 'untouchables' should be physically and mentally clean, quoting Agama Sastra principles for cleanliness. According to the principles of Agama Sastra, the ' chant of Rama' for inner cleanliness and ' a bath' for external cleanliness and those who eat the meat of cattle are not Hindus, and therefore they have no right to enter the temples. Reuben says when malas and madigas convert to Christianity and decide to shun the beef-eating, the upper castes force them to eat the same.
Ramanujam and Reuben believe that the committee activities

against untouchability are not really aimed at the upliftment of Harijans but to protect the Hindu religion from the religious conversions of the depressed. Criticizing Gandhiji's ideology, G. Kalyana Rao gets inclined to the Dalit upliftment programme of Periyar. In order to know why the author gets inclined to Periyar, an insight into the fundamental differences between their ideologies viz., their world outlooks concerning the problem of caste discriminations and untouchability is essential.

Gandhiji on Caste System

According to Gandhiji, there are several virtues in the caste system. His views expressed in 1922 were published in the Navajeevan.

> *"I believe that if Hindu society has been able to stand because it is founded on the caste system. Different castes are like different sections of a military division. Each division is working for the good of the whole ... A community which can create the caste system must be said to possess the unique power of organization... I believe that inter- dining or inter-marriage is not necessary for promoting national unity. (as cited in Ambedkar's writings vol. 9. p. 275 – 276)"*

One can understand from the above lines that Gandhiji had been against inter-caste dining and marriages for some years. Also, Gandhiji had not supported the temple entry of Harijans as their right, arguing just for a few privileges for untouchables. We can understand his perspective from his statement made when a dispute arose between the caste Hindus and the outcasts about the spiritual right of the latter at Guruvayur temple in the 'Ponnani taluk of Malabar'.

During certain hours of the days, the Guruvayur temple should be thrown open to the Harijans and other Hindus, who have no objection to the presence of the Harijans and during certain other hours, it should be reserved for those who have scruples against the

entry of the
Harijans. (as cited in Ambedkar's writings, vol. 5, p. 388)

Gandhiji's views on temple purification after Harijans' visit are as
follows:

> *"I am opposed to purification at all. But if that would satisfy
> the conscience of the objectors, I would personally, in this
> case, raise no objection to purification. (as cited in
> Ambedkar's writings, vol. 5, p. 388)"*

Gandhiji further advises Harijans to view the objections of the
upper castes in an empathetic manner. He says:

> *"The Harijans' attitude should be this, ' if there is a person
> who objects to my presence, I would like to respect his
> objection so long as he [the objector] does not deprive me of
> the right that belongs to me and so long as I am permitted to
> have my legitimate share of the days of offering worship side
> by side with those, who have no objection to my presence, I
> would be satisfied. (as cited in Ambedkar's writings, vol, 5,
> p. 388)"*

Here, Gandhiji does not find fault with the arrangement that the
Hindus have the right to enter the temple on any day and all days,
whereas Dalits would have the right to enter the temple on one
or two days in a year; that too on the condition of the subsequent
purification of the temple. That is why the author Kalyana Rao
calls the efforts of Harijan Sevak Sangh are fake and deceitful.
He conveys this fact through the character of Ramanujam, who
declares that the untouchables do not need both the temple entry
and the subsequent purificatory rituals. Kalyana Rao, being a
revolutionary writer, is aware of the root cause of untouchability.
Knowing that the ownership of land will fetch untouchables a
dignified life, he brings the issue of land reforms before us through

the words of Ramanujam, a member of the Communist Party. Ramanujam says, "No need. No need for their sympathy. It's better to die than live with sympathy. Don't drink. Don't drink water like that. Don't renovate the ruined temples for our sake. If they have a little bit of sincerity in their reform, ask them to do something small. There is a lot of lands adjacent to the mala's mound. The malas and madigas will occupy it. Ask them to watch and keep quiet. That's enough. Gandhiji won't talk about this. These Harijan Seva Sangham workers too won't say a word about this". (p. 196)

Periyar on Caste System

As Ramanujam and Reuben talk about Periyar and the self-respect movement too with enthusiasm, it is needed to analyze the views of Periyar in this context. Ramanujam tells Reuben about Periyar's clarion call that the people should observe August 15 th as a day of mourning. Because Periyar's line of social transformation is different from that of Gandhiji. He declares that "the self–respect movement alone could be the genuine freedom movement, and the political freedom would not be fruitful without the individual self–respect". He sincerely aspired that the caste system vanishes from India.

Periyar believes that the efforts to go back to the ancient traditions of the Hindu religion, as Gandhiji disproportionately opined, cannot ensure individual self - respect and cannot eradicate the social evils from Indian society. He opines that the protection of self-respect is a birthright. It appears that Kalyana Rao acclaims Periyar, who organized the self-respect movement to emancipate Dalits from the pangs of untouchability.

The Lake Water Movement

Yet another most glaring discrimination that has been in prevalence in India is the inhuman hegemony of upper castes over the water resources. Even today, Dalits have been subject to violence when they try to use public wells and tanks in some parts of rural India. Going back to the historical incidents in this regard, B. R. Ambedkar launched a mass rebellion 'Mahad Satyagraha' over the access to Mahad lake water on 20 March 1927. Over three thousand Dalits took part in it to take water from the Chavadar tank in Bombay state as a token of defiance to the existing evil practice of untouchability. Organizing this historic movement, the Dalit activists made rebellious speeches and rallied with the cry of the French Revolution: Liberty, Equality and Fraternity. Twenty people were injured when the demonstration was violently attacked by the police. In 1930, the Communist Party of India officially incorporated the aspects such as the necessity of launching the movements against caste discrimination, the mobilization of Dalit workers to fight against British colonialism etc., in its political agenda. In the same decade, the Congress party and its allied organizations campaigned to facilitate equal opportunities for depressed castes. All India Anti untouchability league under the presidentship of G. D. Birla, with the support of Gandhiji, started working for the well-being of untouchables. The league proclaimed that the depressed castes should access all public utilities like wells, tanks, schools etc. Though the efforts to reform the Hindu religion began even before 1947, the four Varna system in Hinduism has not yet let Dalits achieve equal social status on par with the caste Hindus.

Whenever and wherever Dalits organize movements with the aim of achieving access to public utilities on par with the caste Hindus, the dominant castes and the landlords tyrannically oppress such movements. The state machinery, i.e. the police force too join hands with the landlords in the suppression of Dalits. This unjust social reality is reflected in this novel in chapter: 16. How the upper caste landlords suppress the depressed class and how the state machinery assists them in going against the law are depicted in this novel through the Avalapadu lake water movement of Dalits.

The Village of Avalapadu - The Lake Water Movement of Dalits

The need and dream of Dalits to achieve the right to get access to lake water in villages and the support and efforts of the then outlawed Communist Party in attaining equal rights for Dalits over the public utilities are reflected in this episode. Avalapadu village consists of about three hundred houses. Though there is a lake full of water beside the malas' houses, they cannot step in and take water from it. Holding their pots, they stand away from the lake, waiting for a caste Hindu to pour water into their pots. There is no change in this inhuman tradition even after 1947, in which India achieved Independence from the colonial rule of England. Even if a well is dug there, it will not have any drinking water in it. Hence, except for the lake, there is no other alternative for Dalits in the village.

What the new development in the village is that the communists set foot in that village, and the district and state-level leaders begin to visit the malapalli of Avalapadu. When the Party is banned, that palle gives shelter to the main leaders who are incognito. The Party becomes popular among the washermen community and among the poorer reddys too. Ramireddy is one of the important members of the Party. When a meeting in the memory of the Komaraiah's death [Komaraiah was shot dead while organizing a rally against feudal lords in the then Hyderabad State. After that, he has been revered as a revolutionary martyr] is held in the malapalli, the people from malapalli and chakalipalem attend. Some people from Ramireddy's side also participate in the meeting in which Ramireddy speaks. As there is a ban on the communist party, the meeting takes place most secretively. It is in this meeting that the drinking water problem comes up for discussion.

The malas and the washermen with the enhanced fighting spirit among themselves, at last, decide to get down into the lake, violating the unjustifiable restrictions of upper castes. At the same time, the poorer reddys extend their sincere support. This unity among the malas, the washermen and the poorer reddys has become possible through the genuine efforts of the communists. The unity among the three castes represents the unity in the working class. Being scared of this new unity among people, Venkata Choudary, the landlord and so-called village elder, goes to the police station and some more village elders and complain against Dalits. Ramanujam says that 'their going to the police station is their first defeat'. The landlords who have resorted to violence on Dalits with impunity until then do not dare to do so now because of the presence of the Communist Party.

Dalits, who used to stand for hours together at the lake bund for a potful of water, enter the lake in a state of ecstasy. It is their first experience which is so strange. All this appears to the village elders a turmoil, and therefore they begin to feel like the entire world has become upside down. They come to the shore to attack the malas with axes and sticks. However, the malas who do not wait until they are attacked counter-attack the upper caste people and chase them away. The malas try to fulfil their dream -- the dream of social equality. This news creates a sensation in the surrounding areas. However, the upper castes see villainy in the dream of the depressed while the state machinery also joins them to suppress Dalits. The Avalapadu lake water struggle of Dalits in this novel represents the innumerable valiant struggles of the depressed castes in pre and post-independence eras of Indian history.

The State Machinery and the Oppressed

The writer has depicted the atrocities on the lowest of the lowly by the dominant, influencing the police force, one of the various wings of the state machinery. He has also shown how the laws are violated by those who ought to protect them. When citizens and their rights come up for discussion, that discussion is
essentially related to the origin of the state and state violence. Therefore, at least a brief discourse on the emergence of state and state - violence falls under the study and analysis of the researcher. Karl Marx and Frederick Engels declared: "The history of all hitherto existing society is the history of class struggles." (Manifesto of Communist Party, Visalaandhra Pub. House p. 35)
The state has originated with the emergence of classes that have antagonistic contradictions [conflicting economic interests] between them. In Marxist understanding, the state functions as an instrument for the oppression of one class by another. Engels says:

"It [state] is a product of society at a certain stage of development; it is the admission that this society has become entangled in an insoluble contradiction with itself, that it has split into irreconcilable antagonisms which it is powerless to dispel. But in order that these antagonisms, classes with conflicting economic interests, might not consume themselves and society in fruitless struggle, it becomes necessary to have a power seemingly standing above society that would alleviate the conflict and keep it with the bounds of "order"; and

this power, arisen out of society, but placing itself above it, and alienating itself more and more from it in the state. (The Origin of the Family, Private property and the State, Progress Pub., Moscow, 1977, p. 166, cited in Marxist Philosophy: An Introduction, New Vistas Pub, p 170 -171)."

In this way, the emerged state established its control over people based on territory. In order to control its citizens, the machinery of state came into being. The state machinery comprises defence, police, jails and other administrative institutions. The ruling class, in fact, exercises the constitutional authority of the state machinery. When the ruling class was the masters, this machinery was deployed to control, i.e. to oppress the slaves in slave societies, the peasants under feudalism, and the proletariat under capitalism.

Even though all citizens are equal by birth and law, the powerful, including landlords, bourgeoisie, petty-bourgeois class, bureaucrats and other higher officials, influence public administration. That means, while a larger chunk of the population is deprived of their rights, a few dominant people enjoy their rights. The police force is employed in serving the state and its interests. If the state is run and controlled by the socially and economically dominant class, state machinery serves its interests. This undemocratic and unjustifiable socio-political situation existed even after 1947 in which India became independent. The then major political party deserted the

Gandhian political line. That Party seemed to have admired Gandhiji whereas never tried to bring the Gandhian principles [Directive Principles] under courts' protection. In this background of these conditions, the author G. Kalyana Rao sets the episode of the oppression of Dalits by landlords with the help of the police force. He shows how democracy is sometimes transformed into fascism in this episode. The corrupt and oppressive nature of Chettodu, who was notorious as a cruel police officer in those days, is mocked in every possible context by the author in this novel.

When the police action begins in the village, the youngsters like Sinasubarayudu leave the village, and only the older people, women and children remain in the village. About five middle-aged persons stay back to guard the malas' houses. In an unexpected and unplanned attack by Penchili, a constable flees from the village, leaving his gun at the spot and later reaches the police station safely. Penchili, who took the gun, hides it underneath a haystack on the advice of an older man. When he takes the gun into his possession, he does not imagine that this gun issue becomes the bone of contention. When the news of the attack on the constable and snatching his gun reaches the town, the malapalli of Avalapadu begins to appear abnormal. Having regarded Venkata Choudary as a respectable person, the police considered the malas criminals as they stepped into the lake without prior intimation to the police, and thereby they disregarded the law. In this context, Kalyana Rao depicts how the state machinery supports and protects the interests of the dominant class in society. Kalyana Rao writes with sarcasm as:

> *"... that was how the malas committed a crime. They did not inform the police when they stepped into the water. That was how they disregarded the law. ... Venkata Choudary was a respectable person. ... Such a person said that the malas attacked the farmers houses and misbehaved with the women. The big man would not lie. He had self–respect. He was a choudhary. Not an ordinary choudhary. A choudhary*

> *with hundred acres. ... When Gandhiji came to Andhra, he attended almost all his meetings. ... But if he put his self–respect aside and complained that their women were insulted by the malas, the authorities could understand how horribly, how cruelly, how barbarically the riff-raff had behaved. The complaint of the congress supporter Venkata Choudhary who had self–esteem, self–respect, power, and money, moved the authorities&hearts. There was no need to be surprised that it moved them in that manner. (ibid. p. 221 – 22)*"

Assuring the police officers that he would help them get the communists caught, Venkata Choudhary gives valuable information about the banned communists. The gun which is in the captivity of malas makes the lords panic. Furthermore, the malas, who are communists, snatch the gun of the police, and therefore the police personnel consider the act of Dalits quite atrocious. When Venkata Choudhary gives twenty names, including Ramanujam and others, the police officer Chettodu goes along with his personnel to Avalapadu to restore the peace of landlords. 'In the early hours of the day, they eat thirty hens as breakfast and drink thirty bottles of liquor'.

They first go to the school and arrest Ramanujam. When Yelamanda, the school headmaster, asks why they arrest Ramanujam, Chettodu beats with his lathi on his back. Witnessing the rude attack of the police, the other teachers jump over the wall and run away. Later Chettodu and Venkata Choudhary reach the malas' habitat and start to search the houses for the gun, questioning the people. While Venkata Choudhary shows the persons, saying "he is so – and – so's father, she is so – and – so's mother and she is so – and – so's wife", Chettodu tortures those who are shown in that manner even more cruelly. The assault that began at eight in the morning continues till eleven. Breaking up for lunch, he sternly warns them that they should, in the meanwhile, reveal who snatched the gun and where it was hidden.

Sitting under the shade of the tamarind tree, Chettodu once again looks at the list of names and gets surprised after finding the name of Ramireddy. When he wonders about the relationship between Ramireddy and the malas, Venkata Choudhary says that 'Ramireddy is the communist and that itself is the relationship'. He also finds the names of Jala Ramaiah, who belongs to the washerman community and Singaraju, a Kshatriya, on the list. He thinks that Ramireddy and Jala Rammaiah are dangerous people among all.

In a class society wherein several inequalities reign supreme, the ruling class resort to frightening the ruled that is dictated to be submissive to the former. Sometimes the rebels are imprisoned; sometimes, they are subject to physical and mental harassment; sometimes, their property is destroyed, and the final resort is killings in the guise of protecting law and order. One of the forms of state violence mentioned above is reflected in this episode. Following the instructions of Venkata Choudary, Chettodu torches Ramireddy's house, which is filled with grains. They do it to frighten him so that he will not support the malas again. The neighbouring reddys are panicking and run helter-skelter, witnessing all this. The malas tremble, looking at the burning house of Ramireddy. Subsequently, the police arrest Jala Ramaiah and send him away with Ramanujam and Yelamanda Pantulu to Ongole jail. The raid begins again in the evening with the same question, "Where have you hidden the gun? Who snatched it? Where's Sinasubarayudu ?" (ibid)

Chettodu's cruelty appears at another incident also. The birth pains of Sendri, the wife of Subbaiah, start on the day the gun incident took place. While the midwife sits waiting for the delivery, Sendri, suffering from labour pains, receives a blow of the lathi. The midwife also receives lathi blows from the police. When Chettodu orders his men to drive all the people of the palle to the tree, they bring them kicking, not leaving even Sendri, who is suffering from labour pains more severely. They beat men and women, asking the same questions.

The unity and compassion in masses during the troubled times is reflected in Sendri's delivery scene. When Sendri's pains increase, and she slumps to the ground, the midwife asks everyone to stand around Sendri. Despite the lathi blows and other physical assaults, the human hut formed around Sendri does not crumble. When Sendri and her child are taken to her house, Venkata Choudary and Chettodu cannot obstruct her way. Feeling defeated at the hands of women, Chettodu visits his real anger upon the men. Blood oozes from their bodies when he thrashes them. In this context, Kalyana Rao lays bare how caste is deeply rooted in every aspect of social life. He comments:

> *""In this country, the air that one breathes has caste. The water one drinks has caste. The field canal that flows and the land that yields harvest have caste. The school, the temple and the village square have caste. The food one eats, the house one lives in, and the clothes one*
> *wears have caste. The word one speaks has caste. The state has caste; its laws have caste. God has a caste. Devil has caste. That's why that blood flowed like that. The blood that flowed like that too has caste." (ibid. p. 227)"*

It is only on the third day that Sinasubarayudu comes to know about the gun issue. He gets to know the details, and he thinks that Penchil might have taken it and sends a person for Penchili who does not know that police are harassing his people for the gun issue. Having come to an understanding that unless the gun is handed over, the situation worsens, they see that the information about the gun reaches Chettodu. When the police get back their gun, the attack on the palle is stopped. However, fifty people, including Sinasubarayudu and Ramireddy, are arrested in the palle. For about a year, almost sixty people from malapalli go round the court. They do not have enough money to go often to court as they need to do it once a month. Sometimes, Ramanujam, Sinasubarayudu and Penchili need to go to court three times a month.

However, these difficulties do not bother them as their long-cherished dream of generations is fulfilled at last. When they get into the lake and draw water, the landlords do not dare to obstruct them. The struggle for access to the lake water and the fulfilment of their long-cherished dream mirror the rare social phenomenon that takes place in the lives of Dalits. In accordance with dialectical and historical materialism, quantitative changes lead to qualitative changes in social phenomena. When the village, Avalapadu, begins to become a shelter for the members of the outlawed communist party, the issue of lake water and the deprivation of Dalits remain dormant. However, several incidents which have taken place thereafter lead to the liberation of the lake from the unlawful captivation of the upper castes. Until then, it had been beyond the imagination of anybody in the village that Dalits could achieve equal rights over the lake water. All the incidents --from the event of the commemorating meeting of Komaraiah to the police action on the village-- are all the various incidents and the culmination of all these incidents (which constitute the efforts of people) which are otherwise called quantitative changes, lead to the change of pathetic condition of Dalits and this change itself is nothing but a qualitative change. This social phenomenon was creatively reflected in this novel.

Dalits and the Communist Party

In this novel, G. Kalyana Rao tries to show a solution to the problem of the outcasts who need to achieve equal social status on par with the caste Hindus. Being a Marxist, he expresses his views on eradicating the evil practice of untouchability and privation through the characters of Immanuel and Jessy. The author firmly believes that untouchability, economic exploitation and privation are eliminated only in communism. That is why, though the writer welcomes the attempts of B. R. Ambedkar, a valiant fighter for the emancipation of Dalits from untouchabilty, he believes that the Dalit problem is solved by the efforts of communist-revolutionaries only. Reuben is a sympathizer of the communist party. His son Immanuel is a Naxalite who becomes a martyr in the Sreekakulam peasants' uprising. Immanuel's son Jessy too becomes a Naxalite by joining a communist revolutionary party.

Atrocities of landlords, exploitation of resources by the big bourgeoisie, the privation of the majority of people, hunger, oppression, exploitation and above all, the domination of the upper castes move the heart of Immanuel and make him step towards the Sreekakulam movement. Immanuel sacrifices his life for the people in the Sreekakulam movement. He who went alone comes back as a martyr along with hundreds of people. Reuben, a preacher by profession, says he knows only to send 'God's children, but he does not know how to send 'people's children when thousands of people attend the funeral rites of his son. People. So many people that sand would not slip through. Did not think a death could move people so much. Sorrow in everyone's eyes. Why such sorrow in those faces? What bond was it? What was Immanuel to them? Son, older brother, younger brother, friend .... What was he? Comrade. What meaning did that word convey? (ibid. p. 243)

Immanuel's death moves thousands of hearts. The people bereave at his death as if he were his brother or a friend as he had fought to 'destroy the shameful torture, horrible exploitation and cutthroat culture.' Immanuel and Mary Suvartha's son Jessie grows up with his grandparents and inherits his father's heart of compassion and the determination of his forefathers. His father's sacrifice moves him. He understands that he has yet to read a lot like a man aside3 from the classroom reading. He leaves school and gets into life. He gets among the people who have been the victims of the exploitative and oppressive social order and mingles with them amicably. Besides searching for the meanings of the words -- hunger, untouchability, exploitation, atrocity-- in the 'large expansive school of life', he also searches for their solutions. He, at last, finds the solution to all those problems in the communist revolution. He gets closure to Naxalism and a Naxalite party. We can understand this through the following lines:

"Words. Thoughts. Meetings. Everything a thirst. Everything a desire. Everything a movement. Everything a turmoil. Everything a struggle. Ready to revolt. Jessie would appear like that. Now and then, his friends would come home. Their words would be direct. Would look like arrows taking aim. There would be a lot of arguments between them. They would stop at some point as if they came to an understanding. (ibid. p. 248 – 249)"

Kalyana Rao expresses his anguish on the then-contemporary economic policies of the government during the 1990s in Andhra Pradesh through the conversation between Jessy and his friends. They discuss the oppressive rule of the governments, the hegemonic control of the World Bank on the governments and state terrorism. These governments are completely deteriorating. The leaders' brains have been bought by imperialist government. In this country, every step is targeted to be mortgaged. Our state has gone way ahead on this score. Our government is the pet child of the World Bank. It does not have faith in people. It has no trust in their future. All that is left for them is the police. All that is left is the army. To hunt people. To attack people's movements. To kill the children of the people in the name of encounters. They use people's money only for that. They use the media only for that. That is how their discussions went ... (ibid. p. 249)

They criticize the pro – multinational company policies of the governments in their discussions. They sympathize with the poor who cultivate but do not have 'even a loincloth size of land'. There'll be computers here. There'll be statements of income and expenditure. There'll be groups of multinational companies. These governments say that is, in fact, progress. They are preparing plans only for them. That's not what we have in front of us. The most wretched lives of poverty. They do not have even a loincloth size of land. They don't have jobs worth even old cloth. There's no safety of life in the village. There's no word for the city poor. They don't have their own field, own house or own job. Everything is a life in a dark cave. Hundred years of life was born yesterday and dies today. Using such small words, they were speaking of the state and country! (ibid. p. 249 – 250)

In fact, Jessie joins the radicals after the ghastly Karamchedu massacre in which Dalits were cruelly killed on 17 July 1985 by the upper castes. He joins Jana Natya Mandali, a cultural organization associated with the Communist Party of India (People's War). The killings of Dalits recurred in Aryala, Belchy, Podirakuppam, Kanchkacherla, Keelavenmani in Tamil Nadu and so on. Jessie now begins to sing the atrocities on Dalits. He sings about the houses that were destroyed, the women who were sexually assaulted etc. With this revolutionary ideology, Jessie goes away singing. Yellanna, too, goes away singing, but there is a difference between the two. While Yellanna leaves home without any definite aim, Jessie leaves home with the aim of transforming the unjustifiable society into a justifiable one. He believes that it is possible only through the armed struggle of the oppressed. Jessie becomes a part of the revolutionary movement that carries out the armed struggle with his consort. Though the incidents which occurred during the Srikakulam Naxalite Movement are not narrated, the liberalized and privatized economic policies of the then contemporary governments in the latter half of the 1990s are brought before us in this novel.

The narration of the malas' mound occupation and the Valasapadu barren land dispute reflects the then-contemporary feudal economic and social relations. Furthermore, the justifiable struggle of Martin in the economic sphere has been crookedly turned into by the upper caste landlords as an unpardonable question to their hierarchical social hegemony and whereby they instigate the other caste - people to plunge the lowest of the lowly in bloodshed. Here, we cannotice that even the slightest change in the base causes a commotion in the existing aspects of the superstructure, i.e., the spheres of politics and the religion whose by-product is the caste system. An economic dispute is transformed into a religious one, which has been achieved by the propertied class who had the political hegemony in that vicinity by provoking and intensifying the senseless religious chauvinism among the caste Hindus, who are also part and parcel of the proletariat. Here, aside from the relationship between the base and superstructure, the relationship among the aspects of superstructure also manifest themselves in this episode.

Though the dispossessed struggle for land for cultivation has not lost its relevance in the 1990s, the imperialist economic exploitation, welcomed and backed up by the then-contemporary government, has surfaced as a highly appalling problem in Telugu society. While Naganna and Martin are compelled to acquire land to escape hunger, Jessie and Ruby drift towards the revolutionary movement to liberate themselves from deprivation and the affliction of their long-existing humiliating sub-human status in society. In essence, this novel has reflected the historically evolutionary changes in people production relations, mainly focusing on the material conditions of the social life of Dalits.

CHAPTER FOUR

Untouchable: A Novel of Social Realism With A Mere Modern Technological

It is with Mulk Raj Anand that the downtrodden become the protagonists in Indian English novels, and the themes of stories are chosen from the horrendous living conditions of the lowest of the lowly. The Indian English novel that had been mired in the romantic themes of the high origin is brought back by Mulk Raj to the hard realities of the present-day society. His novels explore the crisis laden lives of the peasants, the discriminative caste system, the inhuman practice of untouchability, the hunger and privation mainly resulting from exploitation of labour, the wretchedness of the poor and so on. These problems of the depressed class in his novels result either from the exploitation by the capitalists or by the feudal lords or by the impact of industrialization on the traditional and agricultural way of life. Even if the problems being confronted by Bakha in his debut novel Untouchable (1935) appeared to have originated from the deep-rooted feudal culture in society, the primary cause behind all those troubles and tribulations is the economic exploitation in the guise of cultural restrictions. In his Untouchable, he voices against the evils of the caste system, exposing the socio-economic problems -- humiliations, hunger, acute poverty of an untouchable family. The story of the novel is set up in the 1930s of Indian society, which had then been entering slowly into the historical phase of capitalism. Even in the new millennium in which industrialization speeded up, the majority of the populace has not been able to get rid of feudal orthodoxy [heartless values] regardless of their religion.

Few Indian novels, before Untouchable, exposed the miserable conditions of an untouchable in the caste-ridden Hindu society. In addition to the untouchable castes like bhangi, chamar, washerman etc., Mohammadans and the English were also considered untouchables in India during the pre-independence period. However, the condition of bhanghi and chamar castes, which were engaged in scavenging and leather works respectively, was too miserable, out of all other castes. G.S. Balarama Gupta says:

> "*The condition of the untouchables in India in the pre – Independence past was no different from that of the American Negro, since he was subject to the same kind of typification that his American counterpart had to suffer for centuries – a typification that spelt deprivation, exploitation and reduction to a part of the myth of the sanskritizing Hindu community. (M.K. Naik. 1985. P. 13, cited from G.S. Balarama Gupta's article "Mulk Raj Anand's Untouchable: The Dialectics of Self – Affirmation").*"

The novel Untouchable exposes the cruel socio-economic chains in which an untouchable youth has been bound since childhood. It also implicitly tells us how four – Varna Hindu caste system suppresses creativity in the lower castes. Even though Bakha is a fantastic hockey player, he is not free from back-breaking inhuman toil to sharpen his skills. M.R. Anand is quite adventurous in his theme for his debut novel in the mid-1930s, entangled in the net of orthodox Hindu religious ideology from which the nonsensical rigid customs originated, existed and influenced the behavioural traits of people in the then society. Commenting on the theme of the novel, M.K. Naik points out:

> "*The main theme of the novel is the age-old inequity unleashed by the traditional and orthodox Hindu community upon a whole class of people within its domain. The preference of theme is a bold stroke of genius. To make a sweeper the hero of his novel is a daring violation of the tradition of nineteen-thirties... (ibid)*"

The problems of Dalits such as poor living conditions, inhuman scavenging work, denial of access to public utilities, humiliations faced by the protagonist in town; sexual harassment on the Dalit girls, bread collection of scavengers during the 1930s in India, the deep-rooted fatalist tendencies in Dalits of the day; protagonist's rebellious nature, internal conflicts among lower castes, and a discourse on the various solutions for the eradication of untouchability specified in the novel etc., are in the vicinity of the researcher's study and analysis.

Poor Living Conditions

The novel, Untouchable reflects how Dalits are deprived of opportunities in the economic sphere of society. This social reality is creatively brought before people through various contexts (episodes). B. R. Ambedkar says, "Untouchability shuts all doors of opportunities for betterment in life for Untouchables. It does not offer an untouchable any opportunity to move freely in society; it compels him to live in dungeons and seclusion; it prevents him from educating himself and following a profession of his choice."

As B.R. Ambedkar aptly describes, the untouchables live in the outskirts of villages and towns in India. They are not allowed to build houses amid the touchable peoples' houses. Untouchables include people engaged in menial jobs like scavenging, leather tanning, and other related works. Even the people who belong to the washer-man community are also considered untouchables. The conditions in which they live are pretty unpleasant and miserable. The poor living conditions of the day are reflected in this novel. S. Sen writes:

> *"The opening scene of untouchable is unparalleled for its realistic touch. Anand dexterously portrays the sordid and ugly aspects of life. Anand believes that beauty and ugliness, cleanliness and filth, sweet and offensive smells go side by side in real life (Sen. 2010. p. 63 – 64)."*

In this novel, Mulk Raj Anand describes the poverty-stricken 'mud-walled houses of outcasts in a heartrending way. Their houses are built with mud located outside the town and cantonment. The untouchables, such as the scavengers, the leather – workers, the washermen, the barbers, the water – carriers, the grass – cutters and other outcasts from Hindu society, live in this locality. The environment in which they live is quite unhygienic and unpleasant.

The protagonist Bakha who is a scavenger boy, lives in a horrible stinking colony. As scavengers are to live on meagre wages and begging, their living conditions are damn poor, and therefore their lives are bogged down in acute poverty. Bhakha's family, which constitutes his father Lakha, brother Rakha, and sister Sohini live in a twelve by five feet single-roomed mud–house which is quite dingy. While Bakha sleeps on a faded carpet spread on the floor in a corner, his sister sleeps on a cot next to him while his father and brother sleep on a broken string bed in the same room. Being the poorest of the poor, they have no other way except to endure the hot days and the cold nights in that room itself. Moreover, as Bakha sleeps with his day clothes on, it is an excruciatingly painful experience during cold winter nights.

Feeling thirsty, after finishing his morning work, he reaches home and looks at the utensils in a corner for something to drink and quench his thirst in vain. He feels like drinking tea. He finds his sister struggling to light the stove. The description of this scene evokes sympathy in readers. There would be no shortage of love and affection among them, even if they were born and raised in poverty. The author describes:

> *"She was blowing hard at it, lifting herself on her haunches as she crouched on the mud floor. Her head almost touched the ground, but each puff from her mouth succeeded only in raising a spurt of smoke and was beaten back by the wet wooden sticks that served as fuel. She sat back helpless when she heard her brother's footsteps. Her smoke–irritated eyes were full of water. She turned and saw her brother. Real tears began to flow down her cheeks. (Anand. p.13)"*

The downtrodden, like Bakha's family, are forced to live in dreadful living conditions. They do not possess proper houses, and the utensils in their houses are not washed regularly because of a lack of sufficient water. As they are not allowed to get water from public wells freely, they do not get sufficient water for their household necessities. This cruel social reality is reflected in one of the scenes in this novel. The utensils in Bakha's house are of clay and have never been washed since Bakha's mother died. As Sohini is young and inexperienced and engaged in backbreaking inhuman scavenging toil outside the house, she cannot devote herself to household work. In addition to this, there is a scarcity of water as, like every 'untouchable', she usually gets a pitcherful of water per day. Because of their profession and filthy surroundings in which they are compelled to live, they require more than a pitcherful of water. Consequently, the aspects such as sanitation, cleanliness, hygiene etc., have not been known to them. In fact, no 'untouchable' family of that era knows them!

The mainstream of society's apartheid outlook makes the untouchables live in miserable and unhygienic living conditions. The basis for main stream's apathy is one of economic exploitation. This is discussed in a later chapter.

Inhuman Job

It is true that the latrine cleaning job is most essential but cleaning the latrines of others is entirely inhuman. Though the latrine cleaning services are among the crucial services, the latrine cleaners fail to get due respect and recognition. They are considered to be mean and heinous by the touchable society. Ramanand, an old moneylender, shouts at Bhaka that no latrine is clean and Bhaka must work for the pay he receives. Bakha bows before him, saying "Maharaj", and later, he runs towards the latrines and cleans the latrines again. His job is quite strenuous. Though he works hard and skillfully, the job he engages himself in does not fetch his honour.

Though being compassionate, Havaldar Charat Sing too does not call Bakha courteously. He calls him a 'scoundrel' in a context. "Oh, Bhakhya! Oh Bakhya! Oh, you scoundrel of a sweeper's son! Come and clean a latrine for me!"(p. 7).
Furthermore, he blames that Bhaka is responsible for his piles disease. He says: "Why aren't the latrines clean, you rogue of a Bhaka! There is no one fit to go near! I have walked all around! Do you know you are responsible for my piles? I caught the contagion sitting on one of those unclean latrines!" (ibid. p.7)

A sweeper's duties involve two daily chores. While the first involves cleaning and collecting the night soil, the latter consists in burning the same. Feeling vexatious of his job, Bhaka does not like to continue as a latrine cleaner, and he would rather prefer to be a street sweeper just like his father as the streets-sweeping work involves the lifting of cow-dung and horse-dung with a shovel and the sweeping of the dust on the road with a broom. It is due to his dislike of his job; he works mechanically.

With his religious perspective, Narendra Modi states in one of his speeches that Dalits have long been engaged in manual scavenging work not for their mere livelihood but with a sense of social responsibility. In his words:

> *"It is a command of God for them to do this job. This work has been in practice in society as a spiritual activity. It cannot be imagined that their [today's scavenging workers] ancestors must have taken up this occupation as they had no other alternative. (Modi. 2007. cited from Telakapalli Ravi's article Mahada Prasthanam, Andhrajyothi Daily News Paper, dated 22 Apr. 2016, print)."*

However, with his pragmatic perspective, M.R. Anand reveals that the people engaged in scavenging work do not find any joy and pleasure. In fact, they try to escape from the cruel chains of such a horrible job. This is reflected in this scene through the inner talk of Bakha. Anand describes the shattered psyche of Bakha as:

> *"Bakha strode along in the open through the stones in the old river – bed that stretched itself between the hills and the barracks of the 38 th Dogras. He felt that he had just invented this business with Charat Singh because he didn't want to go home because he didn't want to see his father, brother, and sister because he didn't want to go and work at the latrines (ibid. p. 90)."*

In fact, no human being chooses this job as there is no dignity in it. Cleaning the excrement of others is quite inhuman. Some people knowingly and others unknowingly question that if nobody chooses this job, how come it is possible to maintain and manage the latrines. In a class society, the poorest will be entrusted with these menial jobs. The caste-ridden class society in India has dictated Dalits to take up this job for their livelihood for ages. This is why Dalits were subject to the deprivation of the right to possess wealth in ancient and medieval periods in India. Therefore, this deprivation has made them accept the mean and heinous jobs. Ranganayakamma, the eminent literary critic, writes:

"Society needs all the jobs cleaning of dirt. But, it is the rule of Hindu society that Untouchables alone should do such jobs. The main source of living of Untouchables is cleaning of the streets and toilets, the burial of dead animals. In some provinces, some laws compel Untouchables to do these dirty jobs. In United Provinces, it was a legal offence for toilet cleaners to refuse to do their work. According to the Punjab police Act of 1911, if a toilet cleaner wants to give up his toilet cleaning job, he could represent the High Court. That was the only recourse available to him. A toilet cleaner going to the High Court! Anyway, it is impossible, so he would be compelled to do the same job throughout his life! (Ranganakamma. 2001. P. 152)."

Hence, Dalits, being the underprivileged, will not be able to liberate themselves from the inhuman and menial jobs until the socialist work division (which cannot come into practice in capitalist societies) comes into practice in the community. In the socialist work division, all are entrusted with both the manual labour and the mental labour, and thereby one particular class or race does not have to engage themselves in menial works for generations together. And it is this system in which the labour values of all, regardless of their caste, creed and religion, will become equal, and this equality will eventually make people shun the senseless practice of the Varna system, a byproduct of religion.

Bakha, being a scavenger boy, confronts several bitter experiences throughout the day. One such experience he undergoes when he goes for the collection of bread from the houses of touchable castes. When he stops at a house for bread (food), the woman of the house yells at him, blaming that he polluted her house. When her child tells her that he wants to go to the lavatory, she says, "No, you can't go. You can't go upstairs; it will lie there all day. Come here, come downstairs, quick and go here in the drain. The sweeper will clear it away" (ibid. p. 64). She does not bother that she is troubling a sweeper during his bread collection time.

This is why Bakha gets horrified by his thought about the prospect of all the coming days of service in the town and the insults that would mercilessly pounce upon him.

The Depressed and Public Utilities

This novel reflects the plight of untouchables, who are restricted and are not allowed to use public utilities such as wells, schools, shops, etc. The author depicts how hard the untouchables struggle to get just one pitcherful of water. After completion of the morning duty, Bakha comes home thirsty and asks his sister Sohini to give him something to drink. Sohini, who goes to the caste Hindus' well to fetch water, fails to get it smoothly as it is not an easy task for Dalits and other lower caste people to get water as they are not allowed to draw water from the public wells. Here, Mulk Raj Anand writes that this social sanction is imposed by 'the Hindus of the three upper castes.' The three upper castes denote Brahmins, Kshatriya and Vysya communities. In this novel, he does not discuss the social status and the right of the upper castes in Sudra castes concerning drawing water from the caste Hindu well. In this context, M.R. Anand does not mention that the upper caste Sudras joined hands with the three castes in oppressing the untouchables. He only says the outcasts and the three upper castes leaving the upper castes in Sudra Varna in the discussion. "The outcasts were not allowed to mount the platform surrounding the well because if they were ever to draw water from it, the Hindus of the three upper castes would consider the water polluted" (ibid. p.14).

On a false ruthless notion that the touch of Dalits would contaminate the entire stream, the caste people do not allow them to draw water from the nearby brook. They are not rich enough to get a well dug for them in their locality as it costs them a thousand rupees to dig a well in the 'hilly town, Bulasha'. Therefore, they have essentially to depend on the well of caste Hindus'. They are sandwiched between the oppressive socio-cultural sanctions and the existing economic exploitation.

As they are not allowed to draw water from the public utilities, they have to wait until some generous upper-caste Hindu pours water into their pitchers. Most upper-caste families are rich enough to get the water – carriers every morning for their baths and kitchens and so only a few families that cannot afford water carriers would come to the well. If anybody among them is kind-hearted, the outcasts will get a pitcherful of water. This socio-economic malady dictates the outcasts to depend on the caste Hindus even for a pitcherful of water. This unfortunate social reality had been in existence in India during the time in which this novel was written; this inhuman practice has still been found in some parts of India even today. This social reality is reflected in this episode.

> "*The outcasts have to quench their thirst at the mercy of the caste Hindus. The outcasts have to beg caste Hindus for a pitcherful of water to wet their throats: Oh, Maharaj! Maharaj! Won't you draw us some water, please? We beg you. We have been waiting here a long time, we will be grateful,' shouted the chorus of voices as they pressed towards him, some standing up, bending and joining their palms in beggary, others twisting their lips in various attitudes of servile appeal and abject humility as they remained seated (ibid. p.18).*"

In a context, M.R. Anand depicts how the untouchables are deprived of the right to education. When Bakha wants to go to school, his father tells him that the schools are meant for the touchable people but not for the lowly sweepers. Bakha realizes, at the British barracks, why his father has not sent him to school. Later, he also realizes that no school would give him admission because of the resistance of the parents of the other touchable students. The parents of the other students would not allow their sons to be contaminated by the touch of the low–caste man's sons. Bojja Tarakam, the eminent writer and social activist, writes in his book Dalits and State that even though the British Government allowed Dalits to enter the schools, the caste Hindus vehemently deplored the entry of the children of Dalits, threatening the government that if Dalits were permitted, they would not send their children to schools and this agitation made the Britishers take back their step in the beginning years. This social reality is reflected in this context.

M. R. Anand brings before us another aspect of the frigid feudal ideology that had possessed even the minds of the school-teachers of the day. Bakha, who is treated as a touchable player at hockey, is an untouchable student at school. Bakha understands that the teachers at school do not teach the outcasts as they fear that their fingers that guide the students across the text should touch the leaves of the outcasts' books, thereby being polluted. The writer's understanding is that as the Hindu four Varna system is discriminative and cruel, an outcast can never be educated so long as the four Varna system is strictly implemented in society. We can infer this from the futile attempt of Bakha, who intends to study on his own.

The untouchables' ordeal of buying provisions from shops in the market is also reflected in the context in this novel. In the pre-independence era (a few decades even after independence too!), the 'untouchables' are not allowed to buy things from shops in the market. They are not to leave currency coins into the hands of shopkeepers lest his touch should pollute them. The shopkeepers, too, do not touch money without purifying it. This barbaric cultural practice of the day is reflected in the following lines:

> "... *facing the shopkeeper with great humility, joined his hands and begged to know where he could put a coin to pay for a packet of 'Red – lamp'. The shopkeeper pointed to a spot on the board near him. Bakha put his anna there. The betel – leaf dashed some water over it from the jug with which he sprinkled the betel leaves now and again. Having thus purified it, he picked up the nickel piece and threw it into the counter. Then he flung a packet of 'Red–lamp'*

cigarettes at Bakha, as a butcher might throw a bone to an insistent dog sniffing round the corner of his shop (ibid. p. 33 – 34). "

In addition to this convention, there is yet another millstone to the necks of the depressed. The sweepers in those days should show themselves in people's presence as little as possible. That is why Bakha cannot venture to go back to the shop to light his cigarette. Instead, he goes to a Muhammadan worker who is 'puffing at a big hubble-bubble' at his work spot, as the Muhammadans were also considered untouchables in those days.

Besides being subject to the ubiquitous social discriminations, the sweepers are often cheated by shopkeepers who charge the sweepers an unduly higher price to compensate themselves for the pollution caused by business transactions with the outcasts. This social reality is reflected in this scene. When Bakha buys 'four annas' worth of jalebi [an item of an eatable which is sweet], he is ashamed of himself at being seen buying sweets. The shopkeeper smiles faintly at the 'crudeness of the sweeper's taste and his spending four annas on jalebis'. While balancing the jalebis, the confectioner cheats Bakha, who does not dare to question the dishonesty of the confectioner. Bakha catches the jalebi packet when the confectioner throws it. He places four nickel coins on the show – board where the confectioner's assistant stands, ready to purify the coins by splashing some water on them.

Mulk Raj Anand depicts several social sanctions on the sweepers. In addition to the caste Hindu well and market episodes, there is a temple episode in which M. R. Anand exemplifies the unethical duplicity of the four-fold Varna system. Bakha goes to the temple for cleaning the courtyard. He at once becomes curious about what is being held in the sanctum sanctorum of the temple. "From here, as he lay, he could peer through with his head raised above the marble threshold, lowered by the rubbings of the heads of the devout, and affording a glimpse, just a glimpse, of the sanctuary which had so far been a secret, a hidden mystery to him" (ibid. p.

51).

While the priests sing a song praising the Lord, he hears with utmost reverence. He is profoundly moved and affected by the rhythm of the song. Unconsciously he joins his hands, listening to the rhythmic song. While he is rejoicing the rhythm of the song, he hears someone shouting, "Polluted, polluted, polluted."Getting panicky at first, he realises that his sister Sohini is tried to be molested by the priest. The predicament of the untouchables deprived of their right to access public utilities and the humiliations they were subject to in the pre- independence era is reflected in various contexts in this novel.

Humiliations in Town

Bakha, having nothing in his possession except the latrine cleaning job, is put to humiliations in town. It had been a custom in the pre-independent India that it was the responsibility of the untouchables to announce their approach so that the caste Hindus would not get polluted by touching them. This custom continued to be in existence in several parts of India even after independence. This bitter social reality is reflected in this novel. Bakha forgets this custom for a while when he is in the market street, and consequently, a caste Hindu happens to touch him. He keeps on cursing Bakha:

> *"Keep to the side of the road, you, low–caste vermin!' ... why don't you call your swine and announce your approach! Do you know you have touched me and defiled me, you cock-eyed son of a bow-legged scorpion! Now I will have to go and take a bath to purify myself (ibid. p. 38)."*

Bakha, who got shocked and could not utter a single word, instinctively joins his hands and bends his forehead over them to apologise. However, the touched man doesn't care what Bakha says. Bakha is perplexed and unable to speak coherently and audibly. The man who is not satisfied with Bakha's dumb humility continues to abuse him in a most uncultured and uncivilized language. He curses Bakha as: "This dirty dog bumped right into me! So unmindfully do these sons of bitches walk in the streets! He was walking along without the slightest effort at announcing his approach, the swine!" (ibid. p. 39).

People who gather around also do not sympathize with Bakha. He feels like running away from the touched man and the crowd when they stoke up the anger in the man with their comments. He thinks that he is surrounded by a 'barrier' that is not of a physical one but a moral one. As the so-called morals have long been imbibed in the minds of the oppressed for ages to tread them down, they believe that they are born inferiors, and so they have to bear the oppression. Here the same feeling tied the hands of Bakha to push the crowd and run away. His fatalism makes him tolerate the abuses of the crowd. Meanwhile, when a 'street urchin' comes before Bakha and complains that he has often been beaten by Bakha, the touched man confirms that Bakha is a rogue. Even if Bakha tells the crowd that he has not beaten the child, the people in the crowd do not care about his explanation. They take a sadistic delight in watching the episode. It is with the arrival of a 'tonga – wallah' who comes up there driving 'an unsteady old mare' and shouts a warning, the crowd is dispersed. "The crowd scattered to safety, exclaiming a vain abuse, exclamations of amusement and disgust according to age and taste". But the touched man's ego is not satisfied, and therefore abusing Bakha, he commits a physical assault on Bakha by giving a slap. Bakha's turban falls off, and the jalebis in the paper bag in his hand are scattered in the dust. He stands aghast while the touched man escapes from the spot.

Mulk Raj Anand, in this episode, describes the inherent rebellious nature in the hearts of the down-trodden. When the touched man unfairly slams, Bakha's eyes become reddish, and he is ready to take revenge. However, the touched man saves his soul and body from the justifiable wrath of a so-called untouchable by taking to his heels. "The strength, the power of his giant body glistened with the desire for revenge in his eyes, while horror, rage, anger swept over his frame. In a moment, he had lost all his humility, and he would have lost his temper too, but the man who had struck him the blow had slipped beyond reach into the street" (ibid. p. 42).

In fact, it can be inferred that the anger and frustration of the protagonist are of the author himself. The author conveys an essential point that the down-trodden also has the capability to retaliate against the oppression of their so-called superiors if their anguish crosses the drawn lines.

Out of all the members who gathered there, only tonga – wallah sympathizes with him. He consoles him and shares the resentment of Bakha to a certain degree. Besides his physical strength, intelligence, sensitivity and self–respect, he finds himself chained and defenceless because he is an outcaste. Later, when he shares his experience with his father, his father too finds fault with him. Being vexed at the ill- treatment he is subject to, he says he would not go to the town again.

Bakha complains that the caste Hindus are ill-treating even if the untouchables announce their approach by shouting. He tells him about the misbehaviour of pundits in the temple and narrates how rudely the woman of the big house in silversmith's gulley throws the bread at him. Finally, he says that he would never go to the town again. Besides, he submits to cruel and unjust traditions and rituals; his conscience neither accepts nor surrenders to social injustice. On the disturbed psyche of the protagonist resulting from the age-old evil practice of discriminative Varna system, R.S. Singh comments:

He experiences human emotions quite like others, but he is always socially denied opportunities to express them. He forgets all humiliations suffered during the day when he is offered a cup of tea by the Havaldar. But when he is condemned for showing love to the child, he feels damned. When he is slapped by a man for polluting him, he shivers with wrath (singh. 2010).

Commonly, Dalits are subject to humiliations that include physical and mental harassment in feudal societies. These conditions are reflected in this novel in a heartrending manner.

Molesting Sohini: The Duplicity of the Upper Castes

The outcasts remain untouchables in all aspects except in the gratification of sexual needs of the caste Hindus. The upper castes do not feel polluted when they resort to sexual assaults on Dalit women. This social reality, i.e. the general nature of learned vulgarism, is reflected in the novel through the character of pundit Kalinath. When Sohini goes to the caste Hindus' well to fetch water, no passerby heeds her request. Pundit Kalinath, one of the priests and in charge of the temple in the town, happens to come by the way. The crowd of the needy repeat their appeals more vehemently than before. As he suffers from chronic constipation problem, he consents to the beseeching of the outcasts. Sohini, who is in her teens, attracts the attention of Kalinath. He calls her and pours water into her pitcher but asks her to come to his house to clean the courtyard. Sohini, being grateful to him, shyly nods and goes away. When she goes to his house for cleaning the yard, he tries to molest her.

When Bakha asks her, she tells him: "He –e-e just teased me, ' she at last yielded. 'And then when I was bending down to work, he came and held me by my breasts."When Sohini resists, Kalinath, in turn, shouts 'polluted, polluted, polluted'. He blames that Sohini polluted him by touching him. Premila Paul writes about this context:

> *"His cowardly attempt to molest Sohini appears all the more offensive because of his accusing her and her brother of defiling him at the temple when the attempt is foiled. This brings into sharp focus the hypocrisy, the double standards and duplicity underlying the facade of purity and spirituality. It is ironic that the Brahmin, 'the custodian of culture in India' as Trinayya calls him, makes an attempt to violate one of the fundamental codes of culture. The innocent Bakha*

and Sohini become victims of the conventional moral codes (Sen. 2010). "

The distance maintained between the Hindu religious institutions or processions and Dalits was also specified in the orthodox Hindu religious tradition. This inhuman tradition led to several social movements. One of such movements was Vaikom Satyagraha, held in 1945 in Vaikom, Kerala, under the leadership of E. V. Ramaswami Naiker and St. Narayana Guru. Following the shouts of Pandit Kalinath, the worshippers also shout that there should be a distance between sweepers and the temple. According to the Holy Books, while they speak among themselves that a temple is construed to be polluted by a low caste man coming within sixty–nine yards of it, Bakha is actually on the steps. They feel they would need to have a sacrificial fire to purify themselves and their shrine. But none of them could have known that Kalinath tried to molest the sweeper girl. The character of Kalinath has exposed the hypocrisy, hollowness and religious bigotry of caste Hindus. Through this episode, M.R. Anand tries to depict the hypocrisy of the oppressive class.

Bread Collection: A Major Ordeal

The scavenging job is the most menial job which the caste people in society do not choose. S.Sen writes that six thousand years of social tyranny and injustice have left an indelible mark on the untouchable life and psyche. They are in a cul de sac from which there is no escape. Destined to clean dung and live near dung, they have to depend on the mercy of their caste Hindu benefactors. (Sen. 2010. P. 201). Because the wages which the scavengers receive is too low when compared with the wages of the workers in other disciplines. The scavengers during the 1930s and 1940s had to depend on the mercy of people. They receive the leftover food as wages for their scavenging services. Though they work hard, they do not get justifiable wages. These exploitative production relations are reflected in this novel.

After completion of the morning work, Bakha goes to houses for food collection. While collecting food, a scavenger has to undergo several difficult experiences. He cannot enter sub-alleys if any caste Hindu is performing ablutions. He has to wait until the ablutions of caste Hindus are complete. Even if he could enter the alley, he could not approach the houses that were upstairs. Because being an outcast, he cannot insult the sanctity of the houses by climbing the stairs to the top floors where the kitchens are. That is why he has to shout and announce his arrival from the pavement itself.

As there is no reply when he announces his arrival at the first house, Bakha moves forward to another house and announces his arrival saying, "Bread for sweeper, mother bread for the sweeper."However, as none seems to have heard him on the tops of the houses, he shouts again in vain. As his legs begin to ache, he sits down on the wooden platform of a house in the lane, feeling defeated. In his endeavours to collect bread, he almost forgets all his bitter experiences of the morning and gets tired and falls asleep.

Bakha knows well that his place is on the brick pavement on the side of the drain, which carries water from the filth – pipes of all the houses. However, he does not care it for a while due to disgust and fatigue. Soon, he slips into uneasy, half-sleep and dreams. How the traumatic experiences haunt the victims even in their dreams is well depicted in this context through the dream of Bakha. "He was tired and disgusted, more tired and disgusted, for he had almost forgotten the cause of his disgust, his experiences of the morning. A sort of sleepiness seemed to steal into his bones. He struggled hard against it by keeping his eyes open. Then he tightly leaned against it by keeping his huge hall door as a concession to his fatigued limbs". (Anand. p. 59 – 60)

Suddenly, he awakes, and the dream fades out. He knows that it is noon and the housewives sit waiting for the ash smeared ascetics. Meanwhile, an ascetic comes crying 'Bham, bham, bholenath' to a house. On hearing his cry, two women rush to the terraces of their house tops and inform him that they would bring food. But when she gets food for the ascetic, she finds Bhakha's body 'knotted up' on the wooden platform outside her house. Seeing Bhakha at her door, she gets angry and begins to curse him. Bakha gets up abruptly and apologizes to her for his actions. He explains that he shouted for food, but she could not hear him. She does not excuse him. She keeps on abusing Bakha, saying:

> *"But, you eater of your masters! Why did you sit down on my doorstep, if you had to sit down at all? You have defiled my religion! You should have sat there in the gulley! Now I will have to sprinkle holy water all over the house! You spoiler of my salt! Oh, how terrible! You sweepers have lifted your heads to the sky, nowadays! ... (ibid. p. 63)"*

Abusing Bakha, she asks the ascetic to be patient as she would fetch food for him. Here, Mulk Raj Anand differentiates between an ascetic and a scavenger who is a worker. He consciously shows in this context through the characters of Bakha and the ascetic how the latter, who does not take part in the production of production, can quickly get food and honour while the scavengers who toil hard get food hardly. Furthermore, they always receive ill-treatment and humiliation from the caste Hindus. The blind faith in religion and the irrational adherence to the four Varna system [Manu Dharma] make people think and behave in a boorish manner. Ascetics bless them, whereas scavengers clean their night soil. The former is a belief, but the latter is an essential service without which society cannot survive. Still, the scavengers are ill- treated, harassed and humiliated.

Meanwhile, the other woman comes down and offers a 'chapatti' [pancake] to Bakha and a potful of cooked rice and vegetable curry to the ascetic. Being too unkind to Bakha, she becomes generous to the ascetic. While the ascetic leaves ceremoniously, the scavenger boy, Bakha, remained entrusted with a gutter cleaning job. While Bakha is doing the work, another woman flings a chapatti at him. As Bakha tries to catch it in vain, the chapatti falls on the brick pavement of the gully. He picks it up calmly and wraps it in a duster with the other chapatti he received earlier. Here the author is successful in showing how the scavengers are treated on par with animals. Having been disgusted to clean the drain after her ill-treatment, he leaves the place in fury. While going home, he also thinks that he shouldn't have picked up that bread from the pavement. Later he realizes that he has collected only two chapattis with which he cannot face his father, who may be angry with him as he comes home with only two chapattis. As he fears, his father gets mad at him, rebuking that he had brought only two chapattis.

When wedding parties are held, the scavengers, washer men, and others engaged in menial jobs are offered some food items and clothes. On the other days, they are, especially the scavengers, content with the remnants of food of the caste Hindus. More pitiably, every so often, the scavengers get stinking food only.

M.R. Anand's narration of the food collection of scavengers arouses sympathy in the readers. In fact, it is quite an injustice on the part of mainstream society. He explicitly conveys the caste-based economic exploitation that had been prevalent in pre-independent India. The injustice of the meagre wages for the more heinous and challenging job is exposed in this context. The author's comprehension of this pathetic situation in which the untouchables were victimized so cruelly has resulted from his humane and pragmatic world outlook. He depicts the troubles involved in bread collection by Bakha and his siblings in a pathetic manner.

Lakha's Apathy to his Son

While Bakha is rebellious, Lakha is submissive to the current social system. While Bakha is rebellious, Lakha is submissive to the current social system. This is why, when Bakha tells him about his experiences of humiliation in the town, he does not support him; moreover, he too finds fault with his son. Even if food is not sufficiently collected on any day, Lakha finds fault with his family members and shouts at them. This is the reason why Bakha fears to go home after bread collection with just two chapatis. He cannot even venture to tell his father about the priest who tried to molest Sohini as he has known about the usual response of his father in such situations. Ever since his childhood, he has seen his father, who never empathizes with his family members.

When we look deeply into why Lakha does not take sides with his family, we can conclude that Lakha has understood the ruthless power of the oppressive four Varna system by his long experience of life. Opposing this unjust four Varna system, the oppressed people cannot survive. Lakha is a man who has submitted himself to the system and wishes that his progeny too should be submissive to the same. Because, if rebellious, those two chapatis too cannot be available!

Lakha does not want his sons to retaliate against the high–caste men. When he hears his son, who has narrated all his humiliating experiences in town, he inquires whether Bakha, in return, retaliated. When Bakha says he has been sorry as he had not retaliated, Lakha gets bewildered. The oppressed people, just as Lakha, fear to retaliate against the oppression of the high–caste men, obviously for two reasons. First, the scavengers are outcasts, and therefore they are inferiors by occupation. Second, the state – machinery such as police, courts, etc.- is believed to be under the unauthorized control of the high–caste people of the propertied class. The ideology of masters – slaves; superiors - inferiors has been deep-rooted in society. Behind the propagation of this ideology, there is an exploitative economic base from which the exploitative production relations emerge and are established in society. It is this ideology that makes the downtrodden the fatalists who accept their sub-human status in society, believing that it is ordained by God. This social reality is exposed through the character of Lakha. Lakha says:

> "*No, no, my son, no, we can't do that. They are our superiors. One word of theirs is sufficient to overbalance all that we might say before the police. They are our masters.*

We must respect them and do as they tell us ... (ibid. p. 71) "

Lakha also tries to convince his son that some caste Hindus are kind-hearted, telling him how Bakha was saved when he was a child by Hakim Bhagawan Das [a doctor]. Lakha also believes that it is the religion that prevents the caste Hindus from touching the outcasts. Marx opines that religion is the opium of the masses as it soothes their agonized hearts. The situation is different in India's social milieu, in which religion has become a hearth of fire on the hearts of the untouchables. With its double facades, it acts as opium for all, and at the same time, it becomes an oppressive and superstitious tool at the hands of those who are higher than the depressed in the hierarchy structure of society.

Bakha's Rebellious Nature

Unlike his father, Bakha is rebellious. Being an eighteen-year-old young boy, he has a 'smouldering rage in his soul'. It is the age in which one cannot be submissive to the oppressive social system. Here, Bakha's feelings represent the feelings of his entire race. The author describes the feelings of Bakha as: "His feelings

would rise like spurts of smoke from a half-smothered fire, in fitful, unbalanced jerks when the recollection of some abuse or rebuke he had suffered kindled a spark in the ashes of remorse inside him" (ibid. p. 42). Usually, he questions himself that why he is to be so humble. He speaks to himself about the discriminative society.

Why was all this?' he asked himself in the soundless speech of cells receiving and transmitting emotions, which was his usual way of communicating with himself. Why was all this fuss? Why was I so humble? I could have struck him! (ibid. p. 42–43)

Recollecting the incident of the touched man in the market street, he is burst into anger and feels that he could have struck the touched man who slapped him. He recalls the lie of the "mischievous"child and the undue abuses of the crowd which abused him. None speaks for him except the tonga – wallah, who is also untouchable. Bakha believes that they have become untouchables as they touch dung. In fact, this is the opinion of the author too. That is why M.R. Anand gets inclined towards a technical solution to the problem of untouchability in India. Bakha thinks,

> *"All of them abused, abused, abused. Why are we always abused? The sanitry inspector and the Sahib that day abused my father. They always abuse us. Because we are sweepers. Because we touch dung. They hate dung. I hate it too. That's why I came here. I was tired of working on the latrines every day. That's why they don't touch us, the high castes. (ibid. p. 43)"*

Another context wherein Bakha becomes furious is the incident of Sohini's molesting. Knowing that the priest attempted to molest his sister, he gets angry. He gets ready to attack him. "I will kill him if ... The son of a pig! ... I will go and kill him! ... and he rushed blindly towards the courtyard."(p. 54 – 55) However, he cannot hit back the priest. It is due to a conventional barrier that dictates the inferiors to be submissive to their oppressive superiors, Bakha becomes stoic. He cannot transgress the social barriers which the conventions of his superiors had built up to safeguard themselves from retaliations and revolutions. The inferiors in the four Varna system cannot cross the socially drawn lines to avenge the atrocities on them. This is the very inferiority complex that protects the high caste Hindus like pundit Kalinath from the attacks by lower caste people. This is the reason that makes Bakha suppress his anger within himself. Saros Cowasjee writes in this context:

> *"If kindness brings forth gratitude mingled with humility, excessive abuse occasionally helps him regain his strength and self–respect. Twice he thinks of retaliation: once when he is slapped by a caste Hindu and later when a priest molests his sister. As such moments he ppears, we are told, a*

'superb specimen of humanity, his fine form 'rising as a tiger at bay'. But he is a tiger in a cage, securely imprisoned by the conventions his superiors have built to protect themselves against the fury of those whom they exploit. The instinctive anger gives way, and the slave in him asserts itself. Untouchable! Untouchable! (Sen. 2010. P. 115). "

Lorose
Internal Contradictions among the Lower Castes

M.R. Anand depicts the internal contradictions among the lower castes. Even if both the washer-man and the scavenger communities are untouchables, contradictions exist among them too. However, these contradictions are reconcilable or sometimes negligible too. The author exposed these contradictions through the characters of Gulabo and Sohini.

Sohini comes to the caste Hindu well for water and finds Gulabo and other women who have been waiting for some caste Hindu to pour water into their pitchers. Gulabo is envious of the beautiful countenance and physic of Sohini. Furthermore, being a washer woman, she thinks that she is superior to every other outcaste. Because firstly, she claims a high rank in the hierarchy of the different castes among the lower castes. Secondly, a famous Hindu gentleman who had been her 'lover in her youth is still kind to her even in her middle age'. Through the character of Gulabo, M.R. Anand frankly reveals the prevalence of illicit relations of some lower caste people with the upper caste people and thereby interprets that some perverted persons in the lower castes take a sense of pride in themselves for such relations. At the same time, he honours the honesty and chastity of the lower caste women through the character of Sohini.

Sohini belongs to the lowest caste among the outcasts, so she is naturally looked down on by people like Gulabo. Being a beautiful girl, she has become a potential rival to Gulabo, which causes hatred in the heart of Gulabo. Economic factors do not involve the contradiction between Sohini and Gulabo; this is a reconcilable contradiction.

Gulabo also comments on the attire of Sohini. She exclaims to Waziro, a weaver's wife, that Sohini goes about without an apron over her head all day in town and the cantonment. Being aware of the vulgar tongue of Gulabo, Waziro pretends to be shocked and unwillingly answers that Sohini ought to be ashamed of herself. However, she consoles Sohini by winking at her. Sohini laughs, and her laughter stokes up anger in Gulabo. Feeling defeated, Gulabo gets infuriated and begins to curse Sohini. When Sohini laughs still more hilariously at the 'ridiculous abruptness' of Gulabo's abuse, Gulabo abuses her more severely.

When Sohini realizes that Gulabo's anger crosses the limits, she remains silent. Her silence adds fuel to the fire of Gulabo's anger. This time Gulabo tries to pounce upon Sohini.

> *"You annoy me with your silence, you illegally begotten! You eater of dung and drinker of urine! You bitch of a sweeper women! I will show you how to insult one old enough to be your mother.' And she rose with upraised arm and rushed at Sohini. (ibid. p. 17)"*

Waziro runs after Gulabo and holds her back. She drags Gulabo to her seat and appeases her. After a few minutes of silence, sobbing and sighing, Gulabo curses Sohini that it is because of Sohini, she started her day of her little daughter's marriage badly, but no one heeds her complaint.

Here Mulk Raj Anand has mainly taken the two communities -- scavengers and washer-men communities-- to show the social differences that exist in the lower castes. In order to project these differences, he portrayed the character of Gulabo.

Besides disunity, M.R. Anand depicts unity too among the lower castes. He shows it through the characters of Bakha, Ramcharan and Chota. Ram Charan is a washer man, and Chota is a leather worker, while Bakha, a scavenger. Ramcharan, being a washer man, is of the

higher caste among them. Chota comes next in the
hierarchy, while Bakha is of the third and lowest category. However,
these friends, who have banished all the thought of distinction
among themselves, eat together and share their joys and pains.
Bakha shares with his friends the bitter experiences he has
undergone on that day and gets consolation in their presence.

> *""Comrade, we're sorry,' assured Chota. 'Come, be brave,
> forget all this. What can we do? We are outcasts.' He patted
> Bakha comfortingly. 'Come, he consoled again, 'forget all
> about it. We will go and play hockey. Let that
> brother–in–law of a priest come down our street, and we will
> teach him the lesson of his life." (ibid. p. 88)"*

Besides discussing the follies of the dominant castes, the discussion
on the prevalence of both unity and disunity among the depressed
castes is equally imperative for the writer who aspires to contribute
to establishing an egalitarian society. Anand's commitment is
evident in this episode though this novel has no potential to impel
people to change society. The trivial quarrels between Gulabo and
Sohini and the amicable relations among Bakha, Ramcharan and
Chota mirrored the actual social scenario in the caste-ridden Indian
society.

Bakha's Emulation of English Men

According to dialectical and historical materialism, two aspects are
essential, though society has several elements. The former is
primary, and the latter is secondary; the secondary tries to imitate
and reach the status of the primary. The primary is of the ruling
class, while the secondary is of the ruled. The ruled follow the
customs and living styles of the ruling class. This social reality is
reflected in this novel through the character of Bakha. He wears his
attire like an English man and works and sleeps in the same clothing
even if he suffers from bitter coldness during nights:

"The nights had been cold, as they always are in the town of Bulashah, as cold as the days are hot. And though, both during winter and summer, he slept with his day clothes on, the sharp, bitter wind that blew from the brook at dawn had penetrated to his skin, past the inadequate blanket, through the regulation overcoat, breeches, puttees and ammunition boots of the military uniform that clothed him. (ibid. p. 2)"

The style of the attire of Europeans has impressed Bakha's mind, and therefore he looks at the English men with wonder and amazement. He watches the lifestyle of the English and also comes to know that they are superior people. Bakha feels that wearing their dress will make him a superior person, and thereafter he tries to imitate them in every aspect. Moreover, it is the English who treat him as a human being. Jack Lindsay remarks:

"Bakha works at cleaning latrines in the barracks, and the tommies are the first person outside his castes who treats him as a human being. The result is a shock which makes him reconsider what he has previously accepted as a natural and fixed order of things. Thus by showing in one small case of the unintended but inevitable effect of British in dissolving the fixed caste as feudal relations which in other ways it has wished to preserve as the basis of its power, Anand reveals at the outset his mastery of method – his capacity to define the general in particular. Not that Bakha is led at once to direct revolt; Anand never over – simplified the development of character. What has happened is that Bakha adores the soldiers and feels he has acquired some new sort of status with his suit of old European clothes, a gift from the barracks. Still, the virus of change is at work in his being (Sen. 2010. P. 81)."

So, he tries to imitate them in every aspect. He begs one 'Tommy' [a British soldier] for the gift of a pair of trousers while a Hindu sepoy gives a pair of boots. He goes down to the rag–seller's shop in the town for the other items, but he does not dare to ask for the price of goods. So, he only stares at them and says to himself that he would walk like the English and look like a superior.

Not only in attire, but he also apes the English men in other habits. When he knows that they don't like gargling and spitting, Bakha feels ashamed of the Indian way of performing ablutions. He also gets convinced that whatever the English men do is a fashion. He does not blow the tea to cool it, and this is another thing that he learns at the British barracks. That is why he considers his uncle's and father's spattering sips were uncivilized habits and accepts the customs of the English and follows them enthusiastically.

He does not like his street and his town, where the practice of untouchability has crept in every nook and cranny of the social life of people. He cannot be happy even at home, wherein his father stoically accepts the undue dominance of the upper castes. So, he likes only the barracks of English men where he sees another strangeand beautiful world as the persons like Charat Singh do not practise untouchability. They treat him as a fellow being. He becomes highly joyous when Charat Singh sends him to the kitchen for a few pieces of coal. While the caste Hindus indulged in the practice of untouchability and never allowed Dalits into their streets and houses, the English allowed them to enter their houses and kitchens. This aspect of social reality is reflected in this context.

Is Untouchability a Problem of Occupation?

Dalits have been pushed away from the mainstream of society for ages. Neither Christianity nor Gandhian way of resistance nor the modern flush system cannot be a solution to their emancipation because they have been evicted from the mainstream of society as a race, not just as the individuals who belong to other
religions. That is why the practice of untouchability and the solution to it are analysed by the author himself from several perspectives, from the Christian religious approach to the Gandhian

philosophical perspective to the modern technological view.

Untouchability - Christianity

In the initial years, the English rulers and their officials were sympathetic towards Dalits as the English, besides Mohammadans, were also considered untouchables in those days. Therefore, the English had to hire Dalits as their servants for their household works. In addition to this, they also allowed Dalits to enter the churches and pray alongside them. This brought in a significant change in the lives of Dalits, and this change soothes their afflicted hearts. However, the upper caste people too began to embrace Christianity for several reasons. With the presence of upper castes in Christianity, the practice of untouchability intruded even in Christianity, which led to the emergence of social discrimination in Christianity. The Christian population was divided into two sects: the touchable Christians and the untouchable Christians. Though several Christian missionaries came to India and worked for the well-being of the untouchables, they were not able to fetch equal social status to Dalits. Because of this reason, most of Dalits were reluctant to embrace Christianity. This social reality is reflected in this episode of the novel. The religious conversions are intensely discussed in the novel Untouchable Spring, but Mulk Raj Anand does not deal with this issue as seriously as Kalyana Rao does.

Colonel Hutchinson, the Christian Salvation Army chief, moves closely with the outcasts and tries to evangelize them. When Colonel Hutchinson asks Bakha why he is sad, Bakha feels flattered, thinking that he has become the object of pity and sympathy from an 'English sahib'. Bakha knows from his father that Hutchinson tries to convert the outcasts to the religion of Christianity. However, Bakha does not want to leave the Hindu fold.

When Colonel asks what happened to him, Bakha is moved and feels confused and embarrassed by his warmth and kindness. Bakha knows all about Colonel because he lives near the church; he visits his colony now and then and mingles with the outcasts amicably. His commitment as a missionary is unquestionable.

Saying that he is also a human being like Bakha, he asks Bakha to come to his God Jesus. Bakha, asking him who Yessuh Messiah is, wonders whether Jesus is a god-like Rama whom the members of his family and ancestors have long been worshipped. Singing hymns in praise of Jesus, Colonel tries to persuade him in vain. When Bakha asks him again in vain who Jesus is.

Overwhelmed with the words of Hutchinson, Bakha does not understand the meaning of the line "He died that we might be forgiven."He does not make out why the people like him should be forgiven. While Bakha's mind is preoccupied with all these doubts, Hutchinson keeps singing the same bit of song. Bakha feels bored but proud of being with a 'sahib'. Moreover, he likes the trousers worn by the Colonel. When he says that Jesus sacrificed his life for people, Bakha remembers his mother telling about sacrifices generally offered to the goddess Kali. When he asks why 'Yessuh Messiah' sacrificed himself, Hutchinson repeats the same lines.

When Bakha fails to understand this time also, Hutchinson recognizes the perplexed look of Bakha. So he explains in plain words. He says Jesus sacrificed himself out of love for mankind, and he treats both the rich and the poor and the Brahmin and the Bhangi alike. Bakha understands that Jesus does not see any difference between a Brahmin and a Bhangi. When Hutchinson asks him to confess his sins so that he might go to heaven when he dies, Bakha does not 'like the idea of being called a sinner' as he believes that he has not committed any sin so far as he remembered. M.R. Anand, in this context, ridicules the attempts of Christian missionaries to find a solution to the problems which exist in the material conditions of social life.

Along with Bakha, Hutchinson reaches his home where the wife of Colonel with contempt receives Bakha. She curses her husband for his association with depressed castes like Bhanghi and Chamars. "I can't keep waiting for you all day while you go messing about with all those dirty Bhangis and Chamars,' saying this,
she withdrew into her boudoir." (ibid. p.123)

Frightened to stay there for any longer, he leaves the place even if Colonel requests him to come to the church located just beside his house. Her abuse is more painful than the physical violence resorted to by the touched man. The writer's purpose is to reveal the narrow-mindedness of the English people like Hutchinson's wife, who hates to establish a humane association with the outcasts. The plain hearted man, Hutchinson, also aims to convert the depressed into Christianity but has no rational theory to wipe out the untouchability of the depressed castes. He says that Jesus helps both the Brahmin and the Bhangi. In fact, help is needed for a Bhangi. When a Brahmin and a Bhangi are equally blessed by God, Brahmin's superior social status and Bhangi's inferiority are not eliminated from society. That is why M.R. Anand does not advocate religious conversions as a means for the untouchables to achieve salvation from the curse of untouchability.

Untouchability - Gandhiji

As part of showing his readers the failure of religion in wiping out the inhuman practice of untouchability in India, M.R. Anand brings the attempts of Gandhiji before us as Gandhiji represents the Hindu liberal ethical thought. The author opines that even Hinduism cannot show any solution to the emancipation of the untouchables from the pangs of inhuman practice of untouchability.

After leaving the house of Hutchinson, Bakha happens to hear that Gandhiji would arrive in the 'city gymkhana ground'. Bakha comes to know that Gandhiji calls the outcasts 'Harijans'. When he hears that Gandhiji has undergone the hunger strike, he wonders thinking about Gandhiji's fasting as he [Bhakha] himself undergoes fasting several times due to his acute poverty. Mulk Raj Anand satirically mentions Gandhiji's fast unto death agitations in this context. This ironic mention indicates M.R. Anand's lack of interest in such idiosyncratic methods of solving problems.

Hearing about Gandhiji's miracles, Bakha aspires to get a solution to his problem of untouchability. Having come to know that Gandhiji would talk about outcasts, he recalls how some Congressmen came to the outcaste's colony a month ago and lectured about Harijans, saying there was no difference between the caste Hindus and Harijans. Gandhiji arrives and makes a speech. He says that the Indians who demand freedom from foreigners callously suppress their own people, the outcasts.

However, Bakha does not make out anything of Gandhiji's words. When Gandhiji begins to explain his boyhood experiences with an outcaste man Uka, Bakha becomes attentive. Gandhiji says he has not practised untouchability, and he wishes to be born as an untouchable if he has to be reborn. Though Bakha is elated at the beginning of the speech, he later feels blamed when Gandhi ji advocates cleanliness and cultivating good habits for outcasts.

Gandhiji also advocates for outcasts that they should not accept leftover food from high–caste Hindus. If scavengers refrain from accepting the leftovers from the plates of high–caste Hindus, they will have to be starved of food. The way Gandhiji has viewed the grave problem whose roots have been entrenched so firmly in the Indian society lacks practicality. Dalits' deprivation of the right to access water wells and tanks and the maintenance of cleanliness are not in compliance with each other. Similarly, his escaping from the moral responsibility of demanding the caste Hindus pay the scavengers and the other outcasts justifiably for their productive services is inconsistent with his mere "sophomoric" advice of 'not to accept the leftovers'. So, both the pieces of advice of Gandhiji are unfeasible as the cleanliness without water is impossible, and rejection of leftovers would inevitably lead to starvation deaths if this impractical advice is followed as a holy tenet by the depressed. At the end of his speech, he mentions two of his strongest desires —first, the emancipation of the untouchables and second, the protection of the cow. Through the Gandhiji episode, the writer aims to expose the impracticable solution of Gandhiji to the problem of the victims of untouchability. S.Sen writes:

"

Gandhi's appearance in the novel stands for solution to the

problem of
untouchability. Anand seems to be motivated by a missionary zeal to
improve society and abolish and eradicate untouchability. But Gandhi
does not play any significant role in their emancipation (Sen. 2010. P.
131). "

Gandhiji's sympathetic words could not console Bakha. Furthermore, he gets startledat the words of Gandhiji, who tells about a Brahmin youth who does scavenging workin his 'Ashram'. He fears whether Gandhiji means that he (Bakha) should keep working as scavengers throughout his life. Unlike the intelligentsia, the masses of India could not appreciate the Gandhian way of struggles as a solution to the problems they confront in their daily lives. The author shows this through the endeavours of Bakha, who is in search of a road by which he aspires to achieve liberation from the heinous latrine cleaning job cruelly inflicted upon him by the age-old oppressive caste system.

Untouchability - Technology

Though disillusioned and disappointed with the speech of Gandhiji, Bakha becomes optimistic hearing the words of Iqbal Nath Sarshar, a young poet in the crowd. He feels assured that he would be relieved from latrine cleaning with the introduction of a machine, that is, the flush system. Being a progressive writer, Iqbal Nath Sarshar condemns all social evils, particularly untouchability. Having been optimistic, he anticipates that the evil of untouchability will be abolished in the future. He stresses the need to modernise Indian society by introducing the latest science and technology and replacing the conventional tools with more sophisticated ones. According to him, machines can bring 'more awareness, self–respect and dignity'. He emphasizes the usage of machines by people to clean filth and latrines. He believes the machines would free the untouchables from the stigma of untouchability.

Mulk Raj Anand shows a solution to the physical hardships of scavengers through the character of Iqbal Nath, who mentions the flush system of latrines so that the scavengers do not have to handle night soil with brooms and brushes and thereby they can achieve emancipation from the cruel clutches of untouchability. In fact, the handling of latrine cleaning duties is not so painful as undergoing physical and mental afflictions, which are depicted with an out and out realism by the author himself. However, he gets inclined to the prospective technological solution. Suppose technology had the potential to bring equality in society. In that case, the people in the developed nations with superior technology could have established at least socially egalitarian societies in their countries long ago. However, the crux of the problems of all inequalities in any country lies in the production system of that particular country. The production system is the determiner of the nature and essence of the production relations. Economic exploitation and religious dogmatism are the chief characteristics of feudalism that had been in existence in India when M.R. Anand wrote this novel taking its theme from the then-contemporary history of society. So, it can be inferred from the above discourse that M.R. Anand seemed to have been uninterested in projecting himself as a Marxist, though there was a considerable influence of Marxist ideology on him while he was writing this novel. In fact, had he not been influenced by Marxism, he could not have emerged as a spokesperson for the depressed who have been viciously subject to social discriminations, political oppression and economic exploitation in his later writings.

CHAPTER FIVE

The Grip of Change: A Novel of Social Realism from Democratic Perspective

Sivakami wrote Pazhaiyana Kazhithalum in 1989 and Asiriyar Kurippu in 1997 in Tamil. Later she translated them into English with the title The Grip of Change and Author's Notes in 2006. However, the title on the cover page is The Grip of Change as Author's Notes is a mere explanatory note in which she defends her ideas expressed in The Grip of Change. Sivakami depicts the social relations and grassroots level politics in Tamil Nadu in The Grip of Change. The story is set in the 1970s and the early years of the 1980s. The central focus is on gender inequalities and the atrocities of upper caste landlords in the villages wherein the prevalence of exploitative production relations has been predominant in India, in which Tamil Nadu is one of the states. In order to know the standpoint of the author, the characterization of the major characters such as Kathamuthu, Thangam, Gowri and Chandran is to be essentially studied and analyzed.

Characterization

Kathamuthu

Kathamuthu is a typical parliamentary democratic Dalit leader who works for his community and tries to strengthen his political status and authority by hook or crook. Embedding several paradoxes and internal contradictions, the author Sivakami portrayed the character of Kathamuthu. He lawfully stands in support of his people whenever the ruthless hegemony of the dominant victimizes them; nonetheless, he demonstrates the same supremacy and hegemony on the members of his family, especially on his wives and daughter. He displays an opportunistic tendency when he thought of working with his fellow Dalit trade union leader and nephew, Chandran.

He, being a Dalit Ex. Panchayat President, Kathamuthu, is the spokesperson and saviour for Dalits in that vicinity, but he is an arrogant and ill-tempered man who becomes intolerant if anybody (who approaches him seeking help) questions him. In spite of his arrogance, with his commitment to work for his community, he attains popularity as a leader in Athur and the nearby villages. His first wife, Kanagavalli, is from Puliyur, and they have two children – Gowri and Sekharan. His second wife, Nagamani, whom Kathamuthu takes into his possession, is a Brahman widow. Her challenging conditions have compelled her to settle in Kathamuthu's house as his second wife.

Though Kathamuthu is a popular leader outside, he is an unhappy husband at home as his wives who have a low opinion about him often disregard him. In fact, this low opinion is of the author herself. The author Sivakami scorns the practice of polygamy through the characters of Kathamuthu, Kanagavalli and Nagamani. Kathamuthu lives with two wives, but he is not affectionate towards them, and therefore he receives the same treatment from his wives.

Kathamuthu was often surprised, and at times felt uneasy. At first, when he called them to press his legs, they would shove each other out of the way, literally pulling each other's hair to get to him first. But now – alas! - even after he called out several times, one of them would appear unwillingly as if she had lost out to the other (Siva Kami. 2006. P. 16).

Kathamuthu, being a brilliant speaker and a clever politician, every time he confronts a problem with others, gets over such issues with his diplomacy. When Thangam is beaten by Udayar's brothers–in–law and his brother on a false allegation that she has established a physical liaison with Udayar, Kathamuthu tactfully does not include this point in the complaint. He changes the version that they beat Thangam because she entered the upper caste street. Also, he added that they abused her with her caste name, which is constitutionally a severe crime because if the case results in a caste clash, the punishment will be heavy. Moreover, they (upper castes) cannot get the votes of Dalits. Later, when he goes to the police station, he realizes that the inspector, an upper caste man, is reluctant to take up the case against Udayar seriously. Strategically dealing with the situation, he implicitly warns the inspector that he (inspector) would be in a severe problem unless he files a case against Udayar's wife and brothers – in - law. "what I want to make clear is that, since you are upper caste, if you don't book the culprits, people may accuse you of being biased. That could be bad for your career. That worries me."(p. 22 – 23) Being well acquainted with the Ramayana, the Mahabharata, and Gandhi's My Experiments with the Truth, which are his granaries, he can spontaneously quote from them while his unlettered caste men listen to him with their mouths open.

He quickly reacts and become active in foiling the plots of Udayar. Knowing that Udayar lodged a complaint accusing Thangam of stealing a transistor and a two thousand rupees cash, Kathamuthu immediately posts guards around her hut, thereby foiling Udayar's plot successfully. This is another specimen of his intellectual acumen.

Kathamuthu is against the violent counter resistances to the violence of upper caste lords. When Udayar's men set ablaze the huts of Dalits, the Dalit youth become aggressive and get ready for violent struggle. However, Kathamuthu dissuades them from counter violent retaliation. His shrewd political outlook makes him foresee the future cruel, violent attacks by upper caste people. This is the reason why he does not advocate the violent struggles of Dalits. He is diplomatic in handling the conflicts and can transform the situation and gain something productive from it. Therefore he demands a hike in wages and ten thousand rupees of cash for each burned house in a context.

Though he is committed to fighting for his community's well–being, he is depraved minded. When Thangam comes to his house for protection and justice, he uses her to gratify his sexual needs. On the one hand, he exploits her sexually, and on the other hand, he appropriates her compensatory money and spends it for his family. Eventually, she becomes his third wife.

Kathamuthu's selfish and treacherous nature has known no boundaries. His brother, Kalimuthu, is a rightful share holder of Kathamuthu's house. Kalimuthu sent a thousand silvers [Five thousand rupees] from Malaysia while Kathamuthu was building the house; nonetheless, Kathamuthu disagrees that his brother too contributed to building the house. Refusing to give a share, he necks out his brother from their joint house. However, when Kalimuthu dies, it is Kathamuthu who takes up the responsibility of holding the funeral rites keeping aside the previous squabble. Later, he also arranges the marriage of Chandran, the son of Kalimuthu. When Chandran achieves popularity as a trade unionist, Kathamuthu becomes envious even though he wants to use his (Chandran's) popularity and become an MLA of Athur constituency in the ensuing elections. He also gets lost in imagination that he would ' pulverize' Chandran after he is elected. His characterization is the confluence of both good and bad elements. Commitment to the well-being of his people, male chauvinism, Machiavellian political tactics etc., are evident in his characterization.

Thangam

The character of Thangam represents the millions of agricultural wage labourers who lead lives in privation and insecurity, undergoing horrendous harassment by their employers, the landlords. Thangam is a Dalit widow in Puliyur village. When her husband dies, her husband's brothers force her, but she does not yield to their demands and desire. Consequently, she loses their support in her life and livelihood. She begins to work as an agricultural labourer on the farm of Paranjothi Udayar, who eyes her. One day while she is working in the sugarcane field, he takes her into the middle of the field and commits sexual assault on her. Unable to resist Udayar, her employer, she bears that torture calmly. "I remained silent, after all, he is my paymaster. He measures my rice" (ibid. p. 7).

It is true that Thangam has no sexual liaison with anybody and leads her life lonely without the companionship of any man. Her purity is unquestionable, but because of her poverty, she bears up Paranjothi Udayar calmly. When Kathamuthu questions her why she does not go after someone of her caste people, she says, "Sami, how can you ask me such a question? I did not go after anyone. I am not a desperate woman. I feel so ashamed. It was wrong, horrible ... I gave in to Udayar ... you should abandon me in some jungle, I never want to go back to that village" (ibid. p. 7 – 8).

Unlike several women, Thangam is not pigeon hearted. Protesting the atrocities of upper-caste landlords, she wants to take revenge on those who beat and torture her. Even if she is thrashed almost to death, she doesn't lose heart but seeks justice with the support of Kathamuthu. She has unduly been alleged to have sensual liaison with Udayar, but in fact, she does not go after Udayar willingly, whereas Udayar himself forces her. However, her husband's relatives spread the rumour that she is the 'concubine' of Udayar. When this rumour reaches Udayar's wife, she employs her brothers and the brother–in–law to thrash Thangam.

Rural innocence and naivety appear in Thangam in several contexts. When Kathamuthu advises her to prostrate before the inspector, she does it just before the head constable assuming that he is the inspector. Later, when she meets the inspector, she hesitates to prostrate before him. However, she falls at the feet of the inspector when Kathamuthu hints her to do so. Thangam exhibits her naivety yet another time when Kathamuthu asks her the money given by Paranjothi Udayar as compensation for the violence unleashed on her. When Kathamuthu asks her to lend him five thousand rupees, Thangam unstintingly agrees to give it.

In the same context, she reveals her idea that she does not go back to Puliyur and work for wages there. She asks for Kathamuthu's help in getting her share of land through the Panchayat. She also says that he could help her get a piece of land by which she could manage her livelihood. As she desires, she goes to the court of law and gets her share of the land. But, in her fight for her share of land with her brothers–in–law, she spends the remaining amount of the compensatory money.

Thangam does not sit idle at home and does not make herself a burden to Kathamuthu's family. Working in the field of Kathamuthu, she earns her meal. Even though she has left the village Puliyur and remained with Kathamuthu's family, she does not forget her horrible experiences with Paranjothi Udayar. She is unable to recover quickly from the troubles she has suffered. She hates the memory of Udayar's sexual use of her body and gradually becomes ascetic. We can understand this by the following lines:

Once she used to plait her long hair, but she no longer bothered with that. She pinned it up without any care and covered her head with her sari. When she saw Gowri plaiting her hair, wearing jasmine, painting a perfect circle of red kungumam on her brow and humming along with duets broadcast on the radio, a lightness spread through Thangam's body. But the feeling almost immediately hardened (ibid. p. 87 -88).

Another aspect in the characterization of Thangam is her hesitancy. Hesitancy is her weakness. She is hesitant because of her unsecured living conditions. That is why she gives in to Paranjothi Udayar, and she does the same when Kathamuthu forces her.

Thangam was still lying down on her stomach, and her hair damp with sweat. Kathamuthu bent down, intoxicated by the alcohol and her posture. 'why don't you eat something ? ' he muttered into her ear. She did not answer him. ... and he fell on her.

"'you are like a brother to me ... a brother ...' she groaned, but her eyes remained shut.' 'Okay. Adjust your sari.' He draped it on her (ibid. p. 93)."

The theory of pragmatics asserts that the readers sometimes need to understand the literary texts moving beyond the literary meanings of the words used in the text to understand the author's intended meaning. That means we need to understand the text from the context and background. If we can rationally apply this theory in this context, we can infer that Thangam's silence preceded by her feeble resistance is half consent. Nevertheless, her consent and frailty can be construed as ones that were resulted from her adversity and helplessness. Later on, Thangam settles down in Kathamuthu's house as his third wife. The only difference between Udayar and Kathamuthu is that Udayar keeps her as his 'concubine', whereas Kathamuthu gives her the position of a wife.

The characterization of Thangam is endowed with several ideal qualities such as self-respect, self-reliance, grit and determination, and so on. She displays all the above attributes in various contexts. She demonstrates her quality of self-respect when her late husband's brothers force her. When she is denied her right to get her husband's share of land, she becomes self-reliant by working in Udayar's fields. Her grit and determination are revealed when she rebels against the violent attack of Kamalam's brothers and brother-in-law. Thangam does not sit idle at home even after Kathamuthu accepts her as a third wife; she works in Kathamuthu's fields. In every aspect, she appears relatively ideal in contrast to the other two wives of Kathamuthu.

Chandran

The character of Chandran represents several progressive forces that surfaced during the 1970s and the 1980s in the Tamil Nadu social milieu. This was when the formation of the occupational trade unions by the industrial workers speeded up. This socio-economic transit is reflected in this novel, primarily through the characterization of Chandran, the only son of Kalimuthu. When his mother dies, he comes back to India along with his father from Malaysia. As Kalimuthu has no separate house in Athur, he stays with Chandran in Kathamuthu's house. Both the brothers jointly built the house, but his stay in that house for over three months makes Kathamuthu irritated. One evening, Kathamuthu comes home drunk and quarrels with his brother. In fact, he pretends to be more intoxicated than he actually is. He accuses his brother of having been negligent of family. Because of Kathamuthu's shouting, Chandran, an eighteen–year–old boy, wakes up from sleep and stands there watching his father and uncle. Then Kathamuthu intensifies his quarrel, saying that Kalimuthu has come back to India only for marrying again after murdering his Malaysian wife. Kathamuthu also expresses his contempt, saying that he has been feeding Kalimuthu and his grown-up son since they have come. Having been offended by his words, Chandran retorts him saying that the land in which the house is constructed does not belong only to Kathamuthu, so the house is his grandfather's property.

Infuriated by the audacious answer of Chandran, Kathamuthu kicks him on his face. Blood oozes out from Chandran's nose. Sivakami intends to tell the readers that Chandran, since his boyhood days, has a revolutionary spirit. This spirit of questioning the injustice and uniting the working class appear in Chandran throughout the novel.

Separated from Kathamuthu's family, Kalimuthu and Chandran begin to live in another house in the same village. He joins Sowbagyalakshmi Rice Mill and Ginning Factory. When he narrates the injustice meted out by Kathamuthu to his co-workers, they, in turn, complain about the mill–owner's exploitation. In this context, the author consciously places the so-called demagogic leaders of the oppressed just as Kathamuthu in the class of exploiters. While the property of Kalimuthu is appropriated by his brother Kathamuthu, the surplus-value of the labour of workers is appropriated by the mill-owner. As the workers in other mills begin to form their workers' union, Chandran and his co-workers also start a union. Chandran, being young and educated, becomes their leader.

His Activities as a Union Leader

Being an enthusiastic new leader, Chandran wants to bring in better changes in union activities. He collects a weekly subscription of one rupee from each member and appoints a colleague to maintain the accounts. Chandran, along with Gandhi, tries to educate the workers, but some abandon education after learning how to write their names. Chandran's idea is to educate his co-workers on various socio-economic issues in society. That is why he reads the newspaper aloud after work to bring in class consciousness in the workers.

After the death of his father, the union affairs become his life. Besides strengthening his union, he tries to establish contacts with the workers of other unions in surrounding villages. He understands that most of the unions have become ineffective with caste divisions. His sincerity and commitment help him increase his popularity. Chandran gradually earns the respect and trust of the people of his caste and other castes. Unlike Kathamuthu, Chandran nurtures his associates. He is 'like the banana tree that flourished along with its offspring' in the author's words. Sivakami's socio-political ideas are reflected in the characterization of Chandran, who is considerate and progressive and embodies the aspirations of those who invite justifiable societal transformation.

Gowri

While Chandran becomes a progressive trade unionist, Gowri emerges as a pro proletarian intellectual. Her chief virtues are intellectual acumen, hatred of male chauvinism, constructive, feminist world outlook, honesty, and sacrifice of the pleasures in personal life. She is the woman protagonist in the novel. Being the daughter of Kathamuthu and Kanagavalli's [his elder wife], she grows up in a hostile and ever sizzling family atmosphere. She fears the presence of her father as her father has failed to establish an intimate relationship among the members of his family.

Consequently, Kathamuthu's ill-tempered and aggressive nature causes to form an emotional gulf between the father and the daughter. Her soul urges her to revolt against her father's undue male chauvinistic supremacy since her childhood. The author shows this in various contexts. When Kathamuthu wants to prepare a complaint letter regarding Thangam's case, he calls her to write while he dictates. He says, "In the said Zilla .. said taluk ... said village ..", she changes the word 'Zilla to the district. She also watches her father's face as she read aloud the line, which includes the change. She enjoys having her slight 'revenge' on him, drawing attention to his outdated language.

When Thangam is ready to give five thousand rupees to Kathamuthu unstintingly and spend the remaining amount to file a case to get her share of land, Gowri sympathizes with her. She thinks whether Thangam can eventually get any money at all for herself. She feels guilty when she rejoices at the 'prospect of a new dress' as it has been bought with the funds of Thangam. Being a young girl, she gets puzzled when Kathamuthu asks the shopkeeper to pack three saris. When she understands that the third 'sari' is for Thangam, she feels uncomfortable.

When Gowri discovers that her father is searching for the bridegroom, she becomes pretty nervous, as she is not interested in getting married. Her aversion to the unruly male hegemonic behaviour of her father is transformed into hatred to the entire intuition of the marriage system. As she does not want to suffer at the hands of some man, she hates the idea of her marriage.

Scenes of her marriage ceremony began to float into her dreams. She imagined various faces in the place of the bridegroom. However, when she woke up in the morning, she did not remember anyone in particular. But fear of marriage remained. She hated the idea of it (ibid. p. 94).

This hatred generated in her heart is due to her father's practice of polygamy. The contradictions among the family relationships also make her vexed at the idea of marriage. Entering the college, Gowri feels that she has crossed over human-made boundaries such as her father, her caste and her village and 'merged with the ocean of people. However, she feels depressed whenever she goes back to her village, where her father and caste reappear.

Gowri, like every other human being, feels hurt when she finds herself in privation. She feels ashamed of collecting the scholarship application form for scheduled caste students from the administrative office of the village. Whenever there is an announcement that the scheduled caste students should collect the scholarship amount, she leaves the classroom with 'a body and mind shrinking in humiliation.

The author exposes the existing gulf between depressed castes through an incident in Gowri's college wherein she gets hurt at the insolent remarks of a backward caste student. One day, when a backward caste student returns after getting the scholarship money, she asks her how much she got. The girl answers "For you, it is different.' Gowri enquires doubtfully whether that girl is not from a scheduled caste. Then, the girl says, "Nonsense! I am a Vanniyakula Kshatriya" (ibid. p. 95). As this disrespectful answer stokes her anger, she argues with that girl for her addition of the prefix 'nonsense'. The incidents of this kind also make her think about the need to transform existing social relations. P. Kalaichelvi writes,

Gowri is firm in her conviction that she will not marry and as a ship, she is hopeful that the world is gripping change towards an ideal world of equality for all. In Gowri's world, no male figure other than Sekhar, her brother, Chandran, her cousin, intrudes to disturb her (Kalaichevi. 2009).

That is why she continues her education even after she receives a doctorate. Assisting Chandran in his union activities, she moves beyond the limits of the caste to strengthen the unity among the depressed people. To the extent of the socio-political ideas, we can find an autobiographical element of the author in the characterization of Gowri, who, unlike Kathamuthu, works for the unification of all depressed castes.

Atrocities of Landlords

As most people in the Dalit communities work in the agricultural fields, most of which are under the lawful or the unlawful possession of upper-caste landlords, physical torture and sexual abuse are the common forms of violence and harassment on Dalits. There might be a slight change in the frequency and intensity of violence, but it recurs now and then in several parts of the country, even in the new millennium. This social reality is reflected in this novel. The atrocities of landlords that victimize Dalits are depicted in a realistic manner in this novel. The landlords indulge in wrong deeds; nonetheless, they themselves harass the voiceless for their consciously committed gaffes. The victimization of Thangam reflects this indefensible social reality. Paranjothi Udayar uses Thangam for his sexual pleasures, but when times move against him, he tries to make Thangam entangled in a false theft case.

Paranjothi Udayar is a wealthy upper-caste landlord in Puliyur village. Just as described in the novel, his lands 'go right up to the next village' where Thangam works as a wage labourer. Most landlords assume that not only the land but also the labourers who work in their lands are also their property. That is why they utilize the services of the agricultural waged labourers indiscriminately. They punish them if they suspect the workers to be convicts. Mere suspicion is enough.

Similarly, they don't hesitate to use their labourers for the gratification of their sensual pleasures also. If they resist giving in, they are rejected to work in their fields for livelihood. This is why women like Thangam are often found to give in to the force of landlords like Paranjothi Udayar. Possessing all the productive forces, which include land and other implements, in their hands, the landlords do not hesitate to unleash violence on the working class, which have nothing in their possession but their labour.

While Thangam works on the farm, Udayar eyes her. In this context, how the dominant in society form a low opinion and how they venture to conduct atrocities on the lowest of the lowly are reflected. According to the view of Udayar, Thangam is 'no princess or minister's daughter'. He also thinks that even if he imposes himself on her, nobody will come to rescue her and further, she is only a lower caste labourer. Therefore, he does not feel restrained in any way, and so one day, ascertaining that nobody is there to watch him, he calls Thangam while she is working alone in the field. He asks her to switch off the water pump and search for the 'hoe' in the sugarcane field. Being unaware of his malicious intention, she goes deeper into the field. While she is in the middle of the dense sugarcane field, he reaches her and drives her to the centre of the field so that none can see them and commits sexual assault on her.

Despite her protests, he overpowered her and pushed her down. She resisted him stubbornly. Her resistance only excited him further. Forcefully he subdued her. Though she had spent her three years of widowhood untouched by a man, she hated succumbing to the loathsome old man's lust. She sobbed with anger sitting in the field (Siva Kami. p. 33).

As Udayar is her paymaster, Thangam is unable to resist him. Therefore, Udayar makes it a routine to have sex with her and satisfy his lust in the pump shed or the fields whenever possible. She can no longer resist him as there is no choice for her. For the unethical action of Udayar, it is Thangam who is subject to physical and mental torture. One day, when Kamalam's brother sees their clandestine sexual relationship and tells his sister, Kamalam, who sends her brothers and brother–in–law to Thangam's house and gets her thrashed with impunity. Though she begs them for mercy, they almost kill her. Aside from the physical assault, they threaten that they would be killed if she stayed in the village.

Even if there is no mistake on the part of Thangam, it is Thangam who receives punishment. The author Sivakami intends to reveal the bitter social reality that if a woman like Thangam had been an upper caste woman, the landlords like Udayar and Kamalam would not have ventured to commit such an assault on her. Dalits and other lower caste people are often put to physical harassment in feudal societies.

Sivakami deliberately showcases the understanding and amity between the propertied class and the state machinery through one of the episodes in this novel. Though crimes are committed by both the propertied and the dispossessed classes in a class society, on most of the occasions, the dispossessed, who are of depressed castes, are sent to jails because of the unethical nexus between the propertied class and the state machinery. This is a bitter pill of social reality to be swallowed. Thangam would have been imprisoned unless Kathamuthu intervenes and foils the plot of Paranjyothi, who is backed up by corrupt police personnel. When Thangam lodges a complaint against Kamalam and her brothers and brother–in–law, Udayar, on the advice of police constables, lodges a counter-complaint that Thangam herself stole a transistor and some cash. He plans to make his false complaint true by planting cash and transistor in her hut. In fact, this idea is given by the policemen who came to Puliyur for enquiry after she complained. This episode in this novel mirrors the prowess of money with which the propertied class can overpower the poor.

Money is not a problem', Paranjothi quickly assured them. 'I'm willing to spend. Please solve this problem for me.' ... one of the policemen suggested to Paranjothi, 'Why don't you lodge a counter-complaint. ... That she had stolen a transistor and two thousand rupees in cash. She's in hospital. You can plant the cash and the transistor inside her house tonight. We'll manage the rest. ... As the two policemen rose to leave, Paranjothi disappeared inside a room. ... He handed one bundle to each policeman (ibid. p. 41 -42).

Knowing about the plot of Udayar, Kathamuthu sends his assistant Subramani to inform Pichapillai to post a few young guards around the hut so that nobody could plant transistor, cash or any valuables in it. In the early hours, two young men are seen approaching the hut by Pichapillai. On seeing them, Pichapillai shouts and alert the guards, who become alert and chase the two young men who belong to the caste of Padayachi. Padayachis also belong to the lower caste and are indisputably a part of the working class. Because of the lack of class consciousness, they join hands with oppressors and are ready to oppress their own class, the working class. Caste consciousness stands as an obstacle preventing the working castes from acquiring class consciousness.

Furthermore, Padayachis are neither at the bottom tier of the caste hierarchy nor at the higher rung. In Marxist understanding, if they can develop class consciousness, they essentially join hands with the lowest of the lowly for social justice. Otherwise, they merely become a tool at the hands of the upper caste landlords and become a part of oppressors victimizing their brethren.

Having been chased by Pichapillai and his men, the two Padayachi young men run back to Udayar's cow shed and gasp in relief. Udayar understands that his plot is foiled; nevertheless, he plans to turn the chasing incident in his favour. He takes the two young men, Arumuga Padayachi and Saminatha Padayachi, to the house of Ramalinga Reddiar while his brother and brothers–in–law accompany him. He cooks a story that the people of cheri unjustifiably attacked the two Padayachi young men. Within no time, several people who belong to upper castes convene at Reddiar's house. The attack on Padayachis for no reason makes them angry, and therefore they together decide not to take Dalits into work in their fields. This episode has reflected the social evictions of Dalits by upper castes that often occur in rural India.

The upper castes decide to hire labourers for seedlings to be planted from the neighbouring village. They also decide to hire Chakkiliyars as there has been hostility between Chakkiliyars and Parayars for the last three years. They plan to keep off Dalits from employment until they come their way, or if they do not give in, they would burn their huts.

'If they don't give in before that, we will burn the cheri to the ground. If the Parayars cannot serve the upper castes, they might as well die,' said Ramalinga Reddiar, the flabby flesh on his chest jiggling.

'Don't say that aloud,' cautioned Paranjothi. ' I am not afraid.' Reddiar pointed to his crotch, ' I can't be shaken.' Fuelled by caste pride, none of them found the gesture obscene. 'Will you stand by that? Don't hesitate' (ibid. p. 50).

As they earlier decided, they set fire to the huts in cheri. First, they set ablaze the hut of Kannamma, and later the flames spread out to other huts too. This kind of atrocity often happens in India. This social reality is reflected in this context. The ultimate violent acts that the upper caste landlords resort to are setting ablaze the huts and killing Dalits.

When Kannamma, whose hut has been reduced to ashes, tells that she has seen a 'man in white vesti and a shirt', people understand that the houses were set ablaze by the upper caste lords. The police personnel and the Tahsildar arrive at the spot. The author, in this context, pinpoints the biased response of the state machinery that stand in support of the propertied class. She expresses her contempt through the murmuring of the people of cheri. People talk about the timely arrival of the police and the Tahsildar, the government administrative official. They grumble among themselves that when Tangam is beaten hard, no one turns up, but now they are present promptly in order to protect the upper caste landlords from the fury of the depressed.

In this context, the author contextually describes the unity among oppressors and their illegal possession of lands, one of the productive forces. The author's understanding is that though there may be disputes among the oppressive forces, they become united to crush the movements and agitations of the ordinary people. They become united to protect their class interests and hegemony. The moment the cheri catches fire, the wealthy Reddiar landlords join hands with Paranjothi Udayar as both of them are equal in number and status in that village. Despite their differences concerning the village administration and political affairs, they timely join hands over labour and wage issues. Being the dominant communities, the Reddiars and Udayars have political nexus with the ruling party so that the ruling party may hardly implement the land reforms. Both the communities have filed a combined affidavit when a case is registered against 'Benami 'holdings, that is, their holdings of lands in the names of others, usually in the names of their faithful servants and sometimes of their pets too.

The Padayachis, who are very strict in observing caste rules, belong to the category of backward castes and have smaller tenements of land. That is why they consider themselves higher than the Parayars and Chakkiliyars. The author expresses her annoyance, commenting that "even the contemporary farmers' movements are also unable to break down the barriers of caste and unite the small farmers of the backward Padayachi community with the other lower-caste communities" (ibid). The hierarchies exist even among the lower castes. The caste-based social hierarchical setup in society helps the oppressive and exploitative ruling classes survive as rulers.

In order to settle the dispute, the officials arrange a meeting in which the upper caste landlords and the victims, along with Kathamuthu and their caste elders, attend. The upper caste lords agree to pay three thousand rupees for each burnt house and hike wages of agricultural labourers from three rupees to three rupees fifty paise and pay one thousand rupees to owners of houses that are partially burned. Along with the increase in wages, the landlords increase the working hours too. They also decide to get a vast Bunyan tree, a public property cut, and sell it out to pay the compensation. However, Arunachala Reddiar is displeased over the decision of raising wages. The conversation among them is as follows:

'We shouldn't have agreed to higher wages.'

'Don't worry. We'll make them work an extra hour. When we pay more, we have the right to demand more work from them.'

'Why did you agree to paying twenty thousand rupees? That's a lot of money,' muttered Ramalinga Reddiar.

'We haven't given in to Kathamuthu's demands, we have only agreed to the tahsildar's suggestion. Later we'll be able to apply to the tahsildar for permission to cut that huge banyan tree next to the school. The auction proceeds will make up for what we are paying now' (ibid. p.75).

The above lines in the quotation reveal the corrupt practices of landlords who are generally obsessed with sermonizing the downtrodden on virtuous qualities.

Unity in Masses

Both unity and disunity exist in the masses who unite on particular issues putting aside their differences sometimes. In The Grip of Change, too, the author depicts the unity and the disunity among the masses. The assault on Thangam makes the residents of cheri angry and tense. All of them respond alike, thinking that the unkind severe assault on Thangam is unacceptable, however much she might be in the wrong. Having learned how cruelly Thangam was thrashed, they resist at heart that the upper caste men should not have entered her hut and beaten hard.

Thangam's relatives malevolently publicize that she deserves that severe punishment as she herself seduced Udayar and committed adultery. Thangam is hurt at their words. The author does not describe specifically why her relatives abuse Thangam. Nevertheless, we can infer that there is enmity between Thangam and her relatives, and the cause for this enmity lies in their production (property) relations. Thangam is refused to be given her husband's share of land by her brothers – in – law who eye her while she does not give in to them.

Moreover, being envious of Thangam's attractive physical appearance, her co-sisters make use of every opportunity to slander her. "That whore thinks too much of herself. She thinks that she's very beautiful. That's why she went after that Udayar. When she loses her shape, he'll throw her out, and she'll be in a state worse than a dog's" (Siva Kami. p. 28).

Although some people sympathize with her, they do not reprimand Thangam's relatives who abuse Thangam. However, they too don't like the attitude of Thangam, who has turned on her sisters–in–law with abuse of her own. Having been offended by Thangam's attitude, even the people who sympathize with Thangam leave her alone, thinking they could talk about the matter the following day. Thangam also forms a sort of aversion towards the people in cheri as they never speak in support of her regarding her husband's share of land. She feels like dejected and lives alone, working on Udayar's land. The village women do not mingle with her amicably, and they avoid talking with her whenever she goes to draw water from the well.

Furthermore, at times when she falls sick, nobody looks after her. Nevertheless, all these contradictions are reconcilable as all [the people in the cheri] of them belong to the same class —-the working class. They should meet their two ends only by working together every day, and therefore the contradictions that exist between Thangam and the village people are temporary. This is the reason why the people in the cheri consider the assault on Thangam unjustifiable.

This unity appears when Pichappillai posts men to guard Thangam's house. Although the young men who guard the hut of Thangam do not have any kinship with Thangam, they carefully guard her hut. The masses who live with differences become united in times of crisis. However, this unity is most often confined within their particular castes in the Indian social milieu. The inspector of Athur police station orders his constables to find facts in Puliyur about Thangam's case. The policemen come to the house of Valliammai, the co–sister of Thangam. While Valliammai is powdering grains, the policemen knock at the door. She comes out and gets frightened to see the two policemen in the front yard of her house. They ask her whether the house is of Thangam's. Instead of abusing Thangam, on listening to her name, she politely answers that they, including Thangam, used to live together in that house a few years ago. She shows them the hut of Thangam, saying "she has been living alone in that small hut next to the school for the last four years". When asked about the relationship with Thangam, she tells them that Thangam is her co–sister. But when policemen ask her what has really happened and whether she knows who beat her up, she cleverly answers that she would call her husband and he would answer their question. She goes inside and informs her husband about the arrival of policemen, and later she goes to Pichappillai to tell about the policemen.

Her husband Manickam, her brother–in–law Sellathurai and her other co–sister Vasantha hurriedly attend before the policemen. Later Pichappillai and others in cheri reach their house. 'In a few minutes, there forms a huge crowd at the entrance of their house'. When the policemen shoot out their questions, Pichappillai takes the responsibility of answering them. While Pichappillai answers, nobody in the people of cheri interrupts him. It shows their respect for their leader Pichappillai and their adherence to the principles of unity among themselves.

When the policemen ask Pichappillai what has happened, he tells them according to the guidance of Kathamuthu. However, when the policemen ask for eyewitnesses, someone from the crowd shouts, 'If you don't believe us, why don't you ask the Chakkiliyars and enquire.' The Chakkiliyars are not aware of the changed version of Kathamuthu. That's why they reveal the truth that Thangam had an affair with Udayar, but they genuinely assert that Udayar's people thrash Thangam. "But we did see those four men hitting her till she bled" (ibid. p. 30).

The timely emergence of the natural unity among the masses is depicted in chapter nine. The author depicts the ability of resistance in them in this chapter. Valliammai is surprised to see some young men occupying narrow cots in front of Thangam's hut and therefore stops there for a while and asks them why they are sleeping there. One of the guards there, Ramachandra, tells her that they are guarding the hut to save Thangam. When Valliammai warns that enmity with Udayar is dangerous, they challenge the atrocious nature of landlords. The youth also condemn the assault of landlords on Thangam; they become enraged at the attempts of Udayar to make Thangam into a thief.

The tenacious young men stay there day and night, guarding Thangam's house. As they chase the men of Udayar the previous night, the Udayar gathers his strength uniting with Reddiars and the other upper castes. The upper castes decide that they should not take Parayars into work in their fields. The unity among oppressors makes the oppressed unite too. In fact, it is essential for the working class, at least for their mere survival.

When the Parayars [the people of cheri] see that the Chakkiliyar women set out for work in the fields of the village, they understand why the Parayar women of the cheri are not called for work. The previous day, both the "groups of women together remove the rice shoots from the seedbed, bundle them and place them in the ploughed fields in readiness for planting them the next day" (ibid). The Parayar women, who were usually called for such work, have risen early and cooked food for the morning and afternoon. They have expected to be called to plant the seedlings. However, they are disappointed and annoyed at the sight of Chakkili women proceeding to work, and so they complain to their community elder Pichappillai.

They talk, shouting about their problem in front of Pichappillai. While talking about the problem, they do not talk about it as if it were their individual problem. They involuntarily begin to talk as if the problem were of the whole cheri.

'This is atrocious, mama! Yesterday they told us to be ready for work and today they ignore us!

' Thatha, why are you keeping quiet? We pulled out those seedlings yesterday, and these women are going to pull out their hairs!'

> "'Look Chittappa, it seems they are hiring workers from other villages for six and seven rupees instead of three, if they can pay double the amount for people from neighbouring villages, why couldn't they have paid us a rupee or fifty paise more?' (ibid. p. 51-52)."

The place is filled with a hue and cry with the women noisily complaining to Pichappillai. The young men like Rasendran, Chellappandi, Chandran too join in with a different set of protestations. They sternly say that the Parayars should never work in the fields of upper castes. They shout that it would be better to die than to work for them. They also propose that if the lords come to them again, they should ask for the same wage they are now paying to the workers from Arumadal and Kilappuliyur. The women also support the proposal of the young men. The author describes the significance of labour in the process of production. She reveals it through the words of a character of an old lady in the cheri. The old lady comments:

'They may own land for miles at a stretch. But the sight of it can be beautiful only when humans toil on it. Can paddy be reaped with the help of magic? They have such plentiful harvests that only elephants and horses can separate the paddy on the threshing floor. They have stored all of it and prospered by selling it for years together ... if we ask for a fifty – paise increase in our wages, they feel that their life will come to an end!' (ibid. p.52).

Pichappillai pacifies and consoles them that the problem would be solved in consultation with Kathamuthu. However, only the bonded labourers go to work in the upper caste households that day. Besides women, men, too, refrain from going to work.

The author believes that all the depressed castes should become one class and fight exploitation and oppression. This idea is revealed through the words of the character of Rasendran. He is one of the young men who guard the house of Thangam. He does not expect that the houses in cheri would be burnt. Earlier, he heard of many incidents in which the people of untouchable castes were burned alive, but he never imagined it would happen in his village. But it has happened in his village too. He understands that the upper castes set ablaze the huts in cheri.

When Ponnusami, a Chakkiliyar, asks why the huts of Chakkiliyar are also burned while there are clashes only between Parayars and upper castes, Rasendran answers that upper castes consider no such division among the depressed castes. Because, even if the depressed classes consider themselves as Parayan, Chakkiliyan, Pallan, Valluvan etc., all of them are untouchables for upper castes. He also tells them that the disunity and internal conflicts among the depressed castes help the upper castes suppress the downtrodden.

"For us, Parayan, Pallan, Chakkiliyan, Valluvan and Vannan may be different. For them, we are all the same – all untouchables. Do you think they would make us stand outside their houses, take you inside, and feed you milk and rice? As long as we continue to differentiate among ourselves and beg for their favour, they will continue to manoeuvre and hammer us into submission (ibid)."

These are not the mere words of Rasendran but also of the author too. In another context, the author also advocates unity among depressed castes through the progressive union activities of Chandran, who mingles with the people who belong to his caste and the people of other castes. He works to promote unity among the working castes to fight exploitation and oppression.

The author opines, in a context, that the Padayachis who are slightly higher up in the hierarchical social ladder (Varna system) are to unite with Dalits. Because both the communities are poor and have similar lifestyles. In support of this argument, the author created two more characters. They are Padayachi woman Lalitha and Parayar man Elangovan. Love sprouts between them, and it is just the love that brings the two different castes closure to each other.

The author's view is those inter-caste marriages in the working castes ensure unity among them. She contends that hierarchies among the lower castes are the major hindrance to the unity among themselves. Pallars are agricultural labourers; Parayars are drummers and menials, and the Chakkiliyars are cobblers. The Pallars considered themselves superior to the rest of them. The Parayars consider themselves higher than the Chakkiliyars, while the Chakkiliyars consider themselves superior to the Para – Vannars, the washer-man community. They wash the clothes of the lower caste, and their women work as midwives for the lower caste women. The upper caste rulers utilise the unequal divisions among the lower castes to suppress and rule the depressed classes. The demarcation among the depressed, whose minds have long been possessed by the devil of Brahmanism in the caste-ridden class society of India for ages, is an inevitable social outcome. This discourse on these inequalities among the lower castes in this context would have been complete if she had further gotten into the root cause of all such social maladies.

Monetary Compensation as a Form of Resistance

The author seems to have agreed to monetary compensation as a solution that compensates victims' humiliation and misery. When the upper castes set ablaze the huts of the lower caste people, three huts in the cheri are entirely destroyed, while two are partially damaged. One Chakkiliyar hut is also burned 'to the ground', and one is partially damaged. Pichamuthu Padayachi's roof has partly been shattered by the fire. Having come to know about this, Kathamuthu arrives in Puliyur. While he is viewing the burned huts silently, the cheri youth surround and pester him that they can see the end of the oppressors if he gives permission. Even Sellamuthu, the community leader after Pichappillai, also expresses his fury similarly before the arrival of Kathamuthu. 'We have suffered enough. Let each man grab a torch or a sickle; let us test our strength!' (Siva Kami. p. 62).

However, the philosophy of Kathamuthu about life and livelihood is different. By nature, he is a Gandhian and can quote Gandhian principles from My Experiments with Truth. He despises Marxism which asserts that the irreconcilable struggle between oppressors and the oppressed is essential until the oppression is entirely eliminated from society. However, Kathamuthu's approach is the one that compromises with oppressors. The author, who often criticises Kathamuthu for his drawbacks, does not fault his compensatory resistance method.

Marxism advocates counter violent struggles to fight oppression, whereas Kathamuthu does not believe in it. Kathamuthu thinks that the victims should make it expensive for oppressors to attack the oppressed another time. That is why, when the youth of cheri is getting ready for counter-violence to teach a lesson to the upper caste landlords who set fire to the huts, Kathamuthu chides them. "While you return with their intestines as garlands, will they be plucking flowers ? Those monsters will swallow you and the entire village" (ibid. p. 65).

It is true that the strength of upper-caste landlords is mighty. Having plenty of resources in their hands, they dictate terms while the people of the working castes obey them. That is why they often resort to violence against ordinary people, especially on the lower caste people. It still happens across the country. Unless the downtrodden give valiant retaliation, they will have to continue to live with sub-human status forever. However, every leader cannot be a valiant fighter. Especially, a hypocrite like Kathamuthu cannot be involved in and lead counter-violent movements because leading comfortable lives cannot get ready to sacrifice their lives. Consequently, they resort to bargaining for better monetary compensation for the loss of lives and property.

Kathamuthu aims to sustain the coexistence of village and cheri but not erase the discriminative line between the two, just as B.R. Ambedkar aspires that the only solution to caste discrimination is the annihilation of the caste system itself in his essay The Annihilation of Caste. Persuading the people of cheri with his argument, he makes them specify and list their demands. Later, he takes part in the talks with the upper caste lords in the presence of the tahsildar and the inspector of police.

While the tahsildar and the inspector sit at the head of the gathering, Paranjothi Udayar and the other upper caste men sit on their right, and Kathamuthu sits on their left. The author could have avoided mentioning the sides on which the two parties accommodated themselves, but she mentioned it consciously. A general perception is that the representatives of the ordinary people are deemed to be leftists while those of the propertied are rightists. With this idea, the author specifically mentioned the sitting places of the landlords and Dalits, who are a part of the proletariat. When Pichappillai and Sellamuthu are about to sit on the protruding tamarind roots, Kathamuthu asks them to sit on a cot. Kathamuthu asks the tahsildar that he, being the injured party, would like to speak at first. In this context, the author Sivakami explains the social disabilities of Dalits. She speaks through the character Kathamuthu:

> *"'... that I was the first one to wear sandals and walk on the upper caste street. In those days, our men had to get off their bicycles as soon as they entered that street and walk the length pushing the vehicle. But I had my hair cut, unlike others, and cycled on their streets" (ibid. p. 67).*"

After the long introduction to the newly changed conditions in villages, he comes to the point of the wages of agricultural labourers. He tactfully turns the discussion towards the hike of wages. First, he raises the issue of Thangam, followed by the huts burning issue. When Ramalinga Reddiar and Arunachala Reddiar protest that they would swear in any temple that they are not responsible for the fire, Kathamuthu expresses his disgust at the interruption. Paranjothi Udayar quietens the Reddiars with a glance. Kathamuthu moves the point that the labourers in Athur and surrounding villages are being paid five to six rupees a day, while the labourers in Puliyur are being paid only three rupees. The horrendous economic problems of Dalit agricultural wage labourers are reflected in this context.

When Udayar asks Kathamuthu to come to the point, Kathamuthu says that the upper caste people set fire to the cheri as they refused to go to work. With the statement of Kathamuthu, Udayar and the Reddiars are pushed into a highly uncomfortable position. The cheri people look at Kathamuthu with admiration and appreciation. Paranjothi tries to argue that they have not called the Parayars to work in their fields in vain. When Kathamuthu immediately hints the tahsildar to ask Udayar why they have not called Parayars to work, Paranjothi Udayar and the Reddiars stutter.

When Kathamuthu demands them to pay ten thousand rupees to each burned house and hike wages from three rupees to four rupees, Udayar replies that they will abide by the tahsildar's decision. The tahsildar proposes that three thousand rupees for the completely burned houses and one thousand rupees for the partially burned houses are paid apart from a hike of fifty paise [half a rupee] in the daily wages of agricultural labourers. In addition to the compensation and the hike of wages, the tahsildar promises the necessary aid from the government side. When the inspector advises Kathamuthu to agree to the offer, he says that he does not have any objection if the government and the elders have decided it. The huts–burning dispute is thus settled.

Thangam's Issue

Kathamuthu settles the issue of Thangam also in a similar manner. After the settlement of huts – burning dispute, the inspector and the tahsildar leave the village. While Kathamuthu is talking to the cheri elders, a message is conveyed to him that Udayar would like to talk to him. He replies to Paranjothi Udayar that he must leave for Athur to go to Trichy to meet the Adi-dravidar welfare officer. He also adds that the Ambedkar Association is organising a procession to the police station to demonstrate against police inaction in the Thangam case.

Hearing the words of Kathamuthu, Udayar gets startled and proposes to settle the issue in the panchayat itself. Kathamuthu asks Udayar to come to Athur to hold a meeting on Sunday. He also requests Pichappillai and Sellamuthu to be present there. The panchayat meeting is held in Athur on Sunday as was previously planned. Paranjothi Udayar, Sellamuthu and the members of Kathamuthu's party attend the meeting.

Thangam hides behind a pillar covering her head with her sari. She does not lift her head thinking that 'she is the origin of the conflict'. A deep feeling of shame causes her to shed tears in silence. She sits through the meeting, wiping her continuously flowing tears. Kathamuthu leads the panchayat along with the representatives of the Ambedkar Association. Getting emotional, one of the Ambedkar Association representatives shouts that it is a severe matter and Udayar is responsible for it. Kathamuthu pulls him back as he does not want anyone else directly confronting Paranjothi. He says that Thangam is a 'poor widow with no children; 'an orphan with no one to take care of her and hence it is proper that Udayar makes her part of his household'. Indirectly, he demands Udayar to marry Thangam. Having got horrified at the proposal of Kathamuthu, Udayar says that he would be abiding by any fair decision or else he should go to a court. Later Kathamuthu demands him to pay Thangam 'ten or twenty' thousand rupees. Udayar agrees to pay ten thousand rupees and pays it then and there itself.

In settlement of both the issues, Kathamuthu tries to penalize the upper castes with some money. He thinks that it should also be expensive for them to crush Dalits again. However much the compensation is lucrative to the oppressed and is costly to the oppressors, it cannot prevent the latter from being cruel to the former, the marginalized.

In fact, this manner of a solution is implicitly supported by the author herself if the text is read in the light of pragmatics. Apparently, there are two causes behind this; first, the impact of the Keezhvenmani massacre and its later consequences; second, the absence of revolutionary movement. The Keezhvenmani massacre of Dalits is to be essentially discussed when Dalit struggles in literature are analyzed. Dalits fought against economic exploitation and social oppression of landlords at Keezhavenmani village in Tanjavur district in 1968. Their justifiable demand for hiking wages caused a furore in the class of feudal lords. The infuriated landlords massacred forty-four Dalits on 25 December 1968 and suppressed their movement. The then ruling party Dravida Munnetra Kazhagam (DMK), was also unable to act in support of Dalits. Media strategically escaped from the responsibility of bringing the atrocities of landlords to the light. Until Indira Parthasarathy wrote the novel The River of Blood, which reflected this bloodbath, the civilized society in the other parts of India did not get sensitized.

This carnage sent a message to the down-trodden that they would not survive if they questioned the hegemony of the upper caste landlords. The Keezhvenmani massacre has resulted from the existing antagonistic contradictions between productive forces and production relations. Following this massacre, the clashes between Dalits and non- Dalits were sporadically occurring in Tamil Nadu. The novelist herself stated in Author's Notes that this novel was written while clashes were occurring between the Vanniyars (Backward castes) and Dalits in the northern districts of Tamil Nadu.

Even though the Naxalbari upsurge took place in 1967, unlike Kerala, Tamil Nadu remained unaffected by the Naxalite movement, which basically aimed to support the lowest of the lowly while trying to mobilize all sections of people. Therefore, the oppressed had no support and protection to resist the oppression and maladministration of the State. Consequently, the violent counter agitation seemed impracticable for the weakest after this bloodbath, and this perception was prevalent in society even during the 1980s when Sivakami wrote this novel in Tamil. The writer's deliberate silence at Kathamuthu's monetary compensation method of solving problems is due to this political environment. In Marxist understanding, ideas sprout from social practice. Here, the writer's view of monetary compensation, a form of resistance, originated from her observation of this stoical socio-political environment in Tamil Nadu.

Unequal Man–Woman Relationships

The unequal relationship between man and woman appears in this novel. The author depicts the oppression of women and criticizes those who fight against the oppression, in turn, suppress their wives at home. Arunima Ray writes in her research article:

When Dalit men, through various ways, try to appropriate identity, they have, of necessity, to fight tooth and nail untouchability itself. Dalit women's case is all the more problematic. They are indeed doubly marginalized; marginalized as Dalits in relation to the 'upper castes' of society on the one hand, and as women within Dalits themselves (Arunima Ray. 2011).

The relationship between Kathamuthu and his wives is an instance of it. Both the wives, who are not much bothered about his contemptuous behaviour, often criticize his ill-mannered nature. In another context, Sivakami advocates inter-cast marriages, especially between Dalits and Padayachis. Even though she describes the oppressive terms between an upper-caste landlord and a Dalit woman, the author's central focus is on the male chauvinism of the so-called Dalit leaders.

Kathamuthu – His Two Wives

Kathamuthu marries Kanagavalli and begets two children. Later, he takes Nagamani to his house and makes her a part of his household. K.K. Pillay explains the practice of polygamy in the Parayan community in his The Caste System in Tamil Nadu. He writes:

> "*Polygamy is in practice among the Parayar. Besides the legally wedded wife, the Parayan invariably had another woman who served as the house's lady. This led to frequent bickering within the family (Pillay. 2007. P. 63).*"

The internal strife resulted from the practice of polygamy by the men in the parayan family reflected in this novel. There are internal conflicts in the household of Kathamuthu too. Because of his ill-tempered nature, he fails to win the hearts of his wives. His first wife, Kanagavalli, being betrayed by her husband, often expresses disgust while his second wife Nagamani behaves disrespectfully. There is no peaceful cohabitation between Kathamuthu and his wives. When Tangam comes to his house for help, Kanagavalli makes scornful remarks on the relationship of Kathamuthu with Nagamani. But she does it as if she were speaking to Thangam. "'Why do you have to spoil someone's marriage? Is that good? You've hurt his family,' Kanagavalli stressed the last part for the benefit of Nagamani, who had come to the verandah with the hot water. Nagamani directed a scornful look at Kathamuthu.'"(p. 7) Nagamani understands that the words of Kanagavalli are aimed at her. She castes a look at Kathamuthu, who in turn shouts at Kanagavalli to bring him coffee. "Are you here to pass judgement early in the morning? Go inside and get some coffee. Now!"(p. 7)

Kanagavalli does not keep silent then. She gives a sharp reply to Kathamuthu, saying that he is not a gentleman to solve people's problems.

In another context, Nagamani too expresses her displeasure over Kathamuthu's crude talk with Thangam. When Kathamuthu asks Thangam why she has not chosen someone in their caste instead of Udayar, she bursts into tears and falls unconscious, moved at the crudity of his remarks. Then, Nagamani comments that he ought not to have spoken like that and rebukes him saying, 'uneducated'. She says, "You don't have to hurt anymore, talking like that. That's the difference between the educated and the uneducated" (ibid. p.8).

Kathamuthu often loses his tongue. He resorts to cutting off cheap jokes and hurting the feelings of others. Usually, there are trivial conflicts with his wives because of his cheap mindedness and loose tongue. His ill temperateness causes a gap between his wives and himself. Instead of love and affection, hostility exists between them, so the relationship between Kathamuthu and his wives is unequal.

Kathamuthu – Thangam

Thangam, who comes to his house for help, becomes his third wife. She does not become a part of his household on the spur of the moment. Like Udayar, Kathamuthu too eyes her when she comes to his house for protection. We can understand the idea of Kathamuthu from his conversation with Thangam. He tells her how Nagamani is leading a secured life in his house. He also tells her that the upper castes use her for their needs, but they would not allow her to step into their houses. Speaking about the attitude of the upper caste men towards the lower caste women, he implicitly advises Thangam to choose a man from her caste to live with. That means he is indirectly suggesting to choose him to live with.

Kathamuthu settles the dispute with Thangam, but he appropriates half of her compensatory money and establishes physical liaison with her. Thereafter, she becomes a part of his household as his third wife. The basis for Kathamuthu's relationship with Thangam, too, is not 'love and affection'. Tangam's necessity of dependence on Kathamuthu makes her give in to him. Furthermore, she has nobody to take care of, and therefore she stays back in the house of Kathamuthu, who shrewdly makes use of her helpless situation and keeps her in the house as his third wife. Kathamuthu's character represents the patriarchal male chauvinism of Dalit leaders at home.

Udayar – Thangam

Though Thangam despises Udayar and her relationship with him, she feels proud when Udayar gives importance to her among other co-workers. Udayar too exploits and 'sexploits' her. When the people of Kamalam thrash Thangam, Udayar expresses his concern just by saying, "They shouldn't have done it ..."But he does not stand in support of Thangam. In fact, he does not want his liaison with Thangam to be revealed to the public as it would hamper his chances to be elected in the ensuing elections. Thangam has no choice. As Parnjothi Udayar is her paymaster, she has no option but to oblige her to pay the master's demand. Lust and helplessness are the basis for the relationship between Paranjothi Udayar and Thangam. So, here also, the relationship between Udayar and Thangam is unequal. Even Kamalam is not an equal partner of Udayar, who was not questioned by the former for his adultery. Instead, she visits her anger on innocent and helpless Thangam. From this unjustifiable act of Kamalam, we can deduce that in patriarchy, even the women in the propertied class have several chains in which they are bound. These are the chains that tie their hands to revolt against the oppressive male chauvinism of their husbands. This is the reason why, instead of questioning or thrashing her husband, she unduly resorts to violence on Thangam.

These relationships are established based on unequal production relations. Kathamuthu and his wives including Thangam; Udayar and Thangam, and Udayar and Kamalam are not equal life partners. The soul and will of these women are suppressed by male dominance. Mini Kapoor says,

> *" "... Kathamuthu is also a patriarch who seeks to completely control the women in his life. There are three of them: his two wives, Kanagavalli and Nagamani, and his almost grown daughter, Gowri. Thangam will be the fourth woman in the household. The money she gains as compensation from her upper-caste oppressors, as well as her inheritance from her relatives, fasten her with Kathamuthu. The three women, having worked through the shakeout of competence posturing, finally find common cause in a patriarchal set up they have made peace with, even as they have learned to fight caste-based inequality" (Kapoor. 2006). "*

Besides the unequal man-woman relationships, the author shows an alternative ideal relationship between man and woman through the characters of Elangaovan and Lalitha. They belong to two different lower castes. The author opines that relationships of this sort can unite the working castes and liberate themselves from discrimination and violence.

Progressive Relationship between Elangovan and Lalitha

The depiction of the relationship between Elangovan and Lalitha reveals the mind of the author, who aspires to see amity and unity among all the depressed castes. Lalitha is the daughter of a Padayachi widow, Mangalavati. Elangovan is a Dalit from Puliyur cheri. He works as a peon in a bank while Lalitha learns tailoring work. Travelling together in the same bus helps them create intimacy between them. They continue to travel together even after the huts-burning incident in Puliyur. The conflicts between Dalits and the upper castes cause a stir in the relationship between Elangovan and Lalitha. While they are travelling, they argue with each other on the huts burning issue, and their argument gradually becomes a minor dispute. While Lalitha supports Udayar, Elongavan sympathises with Thangam. She says that Udayar is a man, and so he can do anything that pleases him. Then Elangovan says whether she would tolerate it if he winks at another woman. She becomes angry at his words and says that he is showing his true colours. Being hurt by her words, Elangovan shouts, saying, "what is wrong with him and what does she mean". Lalitha yells that he has proved his caste. Depressed at her words, Elangovan gets off the bus. Lalitha understands that her words have torn the heart of Elangovan. But she justifies herself, thinking, "How dare he mention winking at another woman to me?"

During their conversation, they address each other as "your people". Though both of them are in each other's love, they still continue to identify themselves as persons who belong to two different castes. Even if they get separated from each other, they become united after a few days, but in the meanwhile, Lalitha had to fight with her mother to sustain her relationship with Elangovan. After the argument with Lalitha, Elangovan avoids going to Athur by bus. He applies for a loan and buys a bicycle. Though Lalitha feels like meeting Elangovan, her pride prevents her from approaching him. Being a conscience-driven woman, Lalitha continues to think over her argument with Elangovan on the bus. She introspects over the incident, and at last, she decides to marry him.

"Didn't I know his caste when I fell in love with him? If I did mind about his caste, how could I be in love with him? How can he not understand that? How many times have I sworn that I would marry only him, even if it meant losing my life! He seems to have forgotten all that. He only remembers what I said about his caste, and that too in a fit of anger" (ibid. p. 106)

In the context of an argument between Lalitha and her mother Mangalavathi, the author becomes didactic, advocating the necessity of the inter-caste marriages among lower castes through the character of Lalitha. Lalitha asks her mother why there should be drawn lines between castes, and she shows an example saying that both Pallans and Padayachis engage themselves in cultivation. She says there is no difference in their pursuit, so there should be no discrimination between them. In the same context, Lalitha reveals that she wants to marry a Parayan. Managalavati harshly responds that if she marries a Parayan, the people will 'spit' on her. However, Lalitha is hopeful of winning over her mother.

Finally, she decides to go to Elangovan and apologize to him. However, that need does not arise as on seeing her, Elangovan receives her with a smile. Both are reunited. The separation has considerably reduced the emotional distance between them, making them determined to marry, setting aside the caste divisions. Through the characters of Elangovan and Lalitha, the author tries to advocate unity among lower castes with an emphasis on the harmony between Dalits and Vanniars. Despite the existence of minor squabbles between them, they still have scope to be united. She suggests that Dalits should join hands with those who perpetrate violence on them. Nevertheless, she ignores the bitter pill of fact that inter-caste marriages are not being held even within the Dalit castes into which Brahmanism has crept and sat with an appalling sturdiness.

CHAPTER SIX

Sangati(Events): A Novel Of Social Realism That Is Confined Only To The Naturalistic Depiction Of The Dalit Women's Problem

Bama's Sangati explores the problems of Dalit women. It is the analysis of Dalit marginalization, gender discrimination and humiliation in the caste-ridden society and a precise record of the tragic conditions of the Dalit women who are doubly marginalized in the patriarchal casteist society of India. The problems of Dalit women are exposed through the anecdotes and memories of the narrator in the novel. The writer mainly focuses on the plight of the women who are harassed and cruelly treated by their husbands, fathers, brothers and landlords. Though her purpose is to lay bare the male chauvinism in society, she, to some extent, brings before us "the harassment of a woman by a woman", which is the chief characteristic of any class society. Depicting the problems of the Dalit Christian women, she tries to explain that the religious conversion also is not a solution to the misery in their lives.

Sangati was written in Tamil in 1994. Lakshmi Holmstrong translated this novel into English and published the same in 2005 with Sangati (Events). The whole narrative is divided into twelve chapters. The word Sangati means events, happenings, news etc. The author portrays the events through anecdotes, memories, and stories in the lives of people in the Paraiya community. Ranjana Singh writes:

Sangati deals with several generations of women: the older women belong to the narrator's grandmother's generation, Velliamma Kizhavi's generation, the downward generation belongs to the narrator, and the generation comes after as she grows up (Singh. 2013).

Gender Discriminations

At the very outset of the novel, the writer criticizes the attitude of the people who are more cautious of the well-being of boys than those of the girls. Though they don't show any difference between boys and girls at the time of birth, they take better care of boys as they raise them. The writer comments on this aspect through the narrator Pathima who says, 'the boys go about bossing over the girls'. Even, Paatti, the grandmother of the narrator, is also no exception for it.

Bama lays bare the gender discriminations that cause misery in the lives of women, especially those of lower castes. How the women of lower castes are subject to back-breaking toil both at home and outside is heartrendingly depicted in this novel. How the more inferior caste women who are cruelly compelled by their basic economic needs would go to work in the fields even during the period of pregnancy is narrated with frightening realism by the writer. By describing an incident, the author conveys the courage of the Dalit women who sometimes deliver babies while cutting grass in the fields.

"...Yes, his mother was out one day, cutting grass for their cow. She was pregnant at that time, nearly full term. She went into labour then and there and delivered the child straight away. She cut off the umbilical cord with the sickle she had taken with her to cut the grass, dug a hole and buried the placenta and then walked home carrying her baby and her bundle of grass. It was only after that they heated water and geeter and gave her a hot bath (Bama. 2005)."

The author also exposes the poverty-stricken lives of the Dalit women who need to work even during their pregnancy through the conversation between the narrator and Patti. When the narrator asks her Paatti why the Dalit women need to go to work while they are pregnant, Paatti says that if they stay at home, they cannot get any food and, therefore, cannot even feed their cattle unless they go to work every day. Even the narrator, too, was born when her mother was working in the fields. Bama explains the prevalence of poverty in Dalits' households through the words of the character Patti in this context.

Another aspect, in this context, the author reveals is that the unjustifiable work division of men and women. Even though the women work as hard as men do, they have to 'struggle to bear and raise children. While men's work ends in the fields, women's work does not finish in the fields. They have to work even at home. Men in the patriarchal society do not share their household work voluntarily. That is why the Marxist literary critic and feminist writer, Ranganayakamma states:

As much struggle is necessary to drag the non-labouring class into labour, as much struggle is necessary to drag the class of mental labourers into manual labour, similarly so much struggle is necessary to drag men into the work of women and to get rid of their male domination. (cited from www.ranganayakamma.org)

It is true that the men who enjoy a comfortable lifestyle cannot liberally lose their supremacy of masculinity. That is why the gender struggle associated with class struggle is necessary for the liberation of women from gender oppression. Cinzia Aruzza opines:

Gender oppression was not merely an economic phenomenon but something that traversed all aspects of social life. It was not only the capitalist who is benefitting from gender oppression but all men" (Aruzza).

The baby girls in a family are discriminated against while they are being brought up. This discriminative family environment forces women to lead lives in hardships since their childhoods. The love and affection the parents give to their baby boys and baby girls are different and unequal. This fact is reflected in a context in the novel through the words of the narrator. If a boy baby cries, he is instantly picked up and given milk, but the same is not the case with the baby girls. If the boys fall ill, the parents take great care, but they do it 'half–heartedly' in the case of girls.

The duration in which a boy breastfed is longer than a girl is breastfed. Gender unfairness appears both at home and outside of it. When the boys become a bit older, they are given more respect. They "eat as much as they wish and run off to play, but girls must stay at home and achieve household duties, cleaning vessels, drawing water, sweeping the house, gathering firewood, washing clothes", and so on.

A line of inequity is drawn between boys and girls even in the choice of games. Girls are not allowed to play the games of boys. Boys don't allow the girls, who are supposed to play games only with stones and shells in the patriarchal society. If girls play the games like kabaddi, they are chided by the elders. Gender discrimination has deepened through every aspect of social life. Women are not born but made in patriarchy as the patriarchal social order moulds them as second-rate citizens.

Another aspect of the gender discrimination reflected in this novel is the unequal wages for the same work done by men and women. Though men and women do the same work and produce the same output, men are paid more than women. The gender-based economic exploitation is brought before us in this context:

The women, in any case, whatever work they did, were paid less than the men. Even when they did the very same work, they were paid less. Even in the matter of tying up firewood bundles, the boys always got five or six rupees more. And if the girls tied up the bundles, but the boys actually sold them, they got the better price (Bama. p. 18).

Though gender discriminations originated long before the origin of capitalism, the capitalist mode of production system uses gender and racial discriminations to enhance the rate of profit and capital accumulation. In patriarchy, though the women as the workers in the fields produce the same output on par with the men, they are underpaid on the excuse that they are women who are wrongly considered that they are not as skilful as the men. This is what is the underlying principle of the gender-based economic exploitation depicted in this novel.

When disputes arise within the community or with the other communities, the community meetings are usually held, but the women are not allowed to take part in them. Dalit elders view that the meetings are meant only for the men. This dejected condition of women is depicted in a context. In spite of the hostility of men, the women pretend to go home but come back in a little while to watch and listen. Again, the women who are crowded over there are abused as 'she – donkeys'. "Will you she-donkeys get out of here, or do we have to stamp on you? The more we drive the wretches away, the more they come back and make trouble" (ibid. p. 23).

When Mariamma is unjustifiably cross-examined and made a victim of male chauvinism and hypocrisy, the frustration and disgust of the Dalit women are expressed in the words of Susaiamma's character. Expressing her anguish, she says that the men would never allow the women to sit down at the village meetings and not even stand at one side. The author ridicules the cowardice of men who suppress the women in their families would quiver to stand and speak before the landlords. The author reveals this fact through the critical comments of Susaiamma. "...But it's only to us that they'll brag. Ask them just to stand up to the mudalaali. Not a bit, they'll cover their mouths and their backsides and run scared" (ibid. p. 24).

In this context, the sexual freedom of men also comes into the discussion. The patriarchal society does not compel a man to be with only one woman, whereas a woman is restricted to live with one man, the husband. When something is accepted and propagated as a virtuous value in society, that particular value should be adhered to by both man and woman. There can never be ethical sanctity to extramarital relations of anyone regardless of their gender. Nevertheless, the point is that the man is tolerated when he crosses the line of cultural restrictions. In contrast, the woman in a similar situation is subject to physical and mental violence. Furthermore, her life is shattered and powdered in the patriarchal mortar if any bad rumour is spread out about her chastity.

The writer depicts the inferiority complex that is deeply rooted in the minds of the women traditionally for ages through the character of Paatti in a context. If she wants to sit at the village council, the village elders too may not object as she has the reputation as a country obstetrician [midwife]. However, she is unenthusiastic to take part in village meetings, thinking that she is a woman who does not know anything and thereby cannot confront men in discussion. She says, "Big woman, small woman, nonsense! Once you are born a woman, can you go and confront a group of four and five men?"She asserts that women, though educated, cannot change the patriarchal social system. When her granddaughter (the narrator) asks whether whatever men say is bound to be correct, Paatti advises women not to open their mouths whether what men say is right or wrong because, if women speak out against men, they are beaten and trampled. The social conditions of women are the same in every patriarchal society. In the same context, the author exposes the contemporary socio-cultural restrictions imposed on women through the character of the narrator, who confronts Paatti with her questions. She asks her why girls are differently treated and brought up, showing the conventions such as the girls are not to talk loudly or laugh noisily; they are not to stretch out on their backs nor lie facing down on their bellies while sleeping and are not to eat before the men in the family have eaten and gone. Representing the women in rural India, the writer brings before us all these discriminative conventions that are still in existence today, though not predominantly.

The anger of the narrator on gender inequality is apparent in several contexts in this novel. Indeed, several conservative restrictions are imposed on women in society. Unlike men, they have to talk in a low voice and sleep, turning to one of their sides. Bama leaves no stone unturned while bringing before us the aspects of gender discrimination in the patriarchal society wherein feudal ideology dictates people's lives. Through the conversation between the narrator and Paatti, Bama tries to sensitize the readers that women are also human beings. In fact, first, they are human beings, later women. Bama shows how male chauvinism has deeply been rooted in society through a song that the lower castes women usually sing. The song given in chapter three reveals the violence and oppression unleashed on women in a conventional patriarchal family setup. The song is as follows:

Crab, O Crab, ...
I Waited and waited for him to come home
And began to eat as he came through the door,
He came to hit me, the hungry brute
He pounced at me to kill me
He struck me, he struck my child
He almost crushed the baby in my womb
He beat me until my legs buckled
He thrashed me until my bangles smashed (ibid. p. 30).

The song conveys that the husband beats his wife, as she has eaten before he does. It is she who catches the crabs in the fields and cooks them, but she has no right to eat them whenever she wants. Karl Marx states that the proletariat is alienated from the products they produce with their labour under capitalism. Similarly, as the poem aforementioned reveals, the contemporary social relations are alienated from the fruit of her toil in patriarchy which is now existing under the protection of capitalism. In Marxist understanding, "a relation of exploitation always implies a relation of domination and alienation".

In this connection, the author tells us through the words of the narrator that "if women are openly seen to be acting in unexpected ways, it is true that everyone will abuse them."It is true that women are not allowed to cross the drawn lines in patriarchy. As the author rightly says, if they cross the lines, they are mercilessly suppressed by patriarchal social order if they act in 'unexpected ways'. Even in the early decades of the second half of the 20th century, men used to beat and kill their wives for trivial reasons or the mere gratification of their egos. This social reality is reflected in this context.

How the Dalit women are subjugated even at the places of spirituality is reflected in the context in this novel. The position of girls is worse at church. They are not allowed to enter the sacristy and not permitted to play the roles (woman roles) in the church plays. Instead, the woman characters, too, are played by men. Gender discriminations continue to be in existence even at church.

The position of women is both pitiful and humiliating, really. In the fields, they have to escape from upper-caste men's molestations. At church, they must lick the priest's shoes and be his slaves while he threatens them with tales of God, Heaven and Hell. Even when they go to their own homes, before they have had a chance to cook some kanji or lie down and rest a little, they have to submit themselves to their husbands' torment (ibid. p. 35).

The Plight of Women at Home

The writer has movingly depicted the predicament of women as the wives and the daughters in a traditional family set up in India through the character of Mariamma, another granddaughter of Paatti. When Mariamma comes of age, she is uncared by her father, Samudrakani. As her mother is no more, her father, a drunkard, cohabitates with another woman. He is gratified as long as his stomach is full and he does not look after his children. He does not celebrate when his daughter comes of age and sits in traditional 'kuchullu' (beginning of the stage of puberty) for eight days.

Further, he does not try to marry her off to some responsible man. When Paatti reminds him about his responsibility, he finds fault with his daughter's character (purity). Having trusted in the story cooked up by the landlord Kumarasami, he decides to marry her off to Manikkam, an out and out drunkard. Mariamma refuses at first but later agrees when her father "badgers and chivvies" to the proposal as she has no other way. However, from the moment she is married, she suffers torture every day. "... Mariamma suffered blows and kicks and beatings every day, and was reduced to no more than a half-life, or even less" (ibid. p. 42). All this happens because of the mischief and cunning nature of a landlord. His lust and crookedness make Mariamma a scapegoat, and thereby, her whole life is destroyed.

A woman's life is destroyed if others slander her. No man will come forward to marry her, whereas if a man has an illicit connection with another woman, society doesn't care, and he is allowed to marry whom he likes. Justice or morality is not the same as man and woman in patriarchy. Furthermore, the woman is forced to marry the man she is said to have a liaison with. This grave social reality of gender oppression is touchingly reflected in this context through the words of the narrator's character. "If a woman is slandered, that's always her fate. People won't consider whether the accusation is true, nor will they allow the woman to speak out. They will marry her off to any disreputable fellow and wash their hands off her, not caring in the least whether she lives or dies" (ibid. p. 42).

The novel Sangati is a collection of several events. While reading this novel, we can understand the writer's purpose behind the writing of this novel. In order to expose the problems of Dalit women, the writer creates characters and weaves the stories taken from contemporary social phenomena. In society, there is a popular notion that a man can beat or kill his wife, showing that the particular woman is his wife. In order to criticize this tendency in patriarchy, the writer has created the character of Thayi, who leads a wretched life being a victim of domestic violence.

Thaayi, the 'lightest–skinned woman' in the locality, is a poor victim of her husband's cruelty. It is due to the force of her parents, and she had to marry him. One day, the narrator happens to see her being thrashed by her husband in the street. When Karuthamuthu comes to rescue her and questions her husband's savagery, he [Thaayi's husband] becomes even more furious and tells him that she is his wife, so he is entitled to beat or kill her. Later, he begins to beat more violently. If anybody intervenes in the situation, he curses her a whore and hits even harder. Through the conversation between the narrator and her mother, the writer unveils the current marriage system in which unequal family relations exist unhindered. The conversation is as follows:

> *"... When I came home, I said to my mother, 'well, Amma, just because he's tied a tali round her neck, does it mean he can beat his wife as he likes? It's just pitiful to see Thaayi, Amma.' My mother sighed and said, 'It's as if you become a slave from the very day you are married. That's why all the men sold their wives and kept them well under control... (ibid. p. 43). "*

When the narrator sees Thaayi, she finds a big bunch of hair tied to the doorpost of the threshold, hanging down. When she asks why that bunch of hair is hanging from the doorpost, Thaayi's husband comes out and says that he cuts off her hair to suppress her pride. This is another form of cruelty and violence. Later, when the narrator asks her mother why Thaaayi should put up her husband's cruelty and why she cannot leave him and live by herself, her mother says that it is not so easy for a woman to leave her husband and live alone in this society. It is the truth that the women who have left their husbands are pestered by the people, especially by their fellow women. "It's not so easy to get away once you are married. Once you've put your head in the mortar, can you escape from the pestle? No, she must continue to suffer until her head rests on the earth at last" (ibid. p. 44).

The above belief is deeply rooted in the Indian culture. Hence, though suffering at the hands of her husband, the woman cannot venture to break the marriage. It is this social reality that is reflected in this context. In addition to the poor women who are the victims of their husbands' cruelty and harassment, Bama tells us about some other women who rise against the barbaric violence of their drunkard husbands. She depicts this kind of incident that rarely occur in society through Raakkamma and Paakkiaraj.

Paakkiaraj, who is a drunkard, beats his wife Raakkamma every day. Unable to bear his torture, she begins to act tactically whenever her husband pounces upon her. Before his hand falls on her, she screams and shrieks, "Ayyayyo, he's killing me. Vile man, you'll die, you'll be carried out as a corpse, you low - life, you bastard, you this you that ..." (ibid. p. 61). One day when Pakkiaraj manhandles her, she challenges him to fight with a man who is of his equal. Her challenge infuriates and provokes him to thrash her more severely. Raakkamma, shouting obscenities, lifts her sari in front of the entire crowd gather there to unnerve her husband and thereby to protect herself from his spiteful assault. All the women who gathered there speak amongst themselves that whether Raakkamma is a woman. However, Raakkamma defends her uncivilized act by answering them sternly that her husband would have killed her if she had not behaved in such a manner. The narrator empathizes with Raakkamma, who shouts, screams and behaves in such a manner. She understands that Raakkamma behaves in such a vulgar manner only to escape from her husband's harassment.

Just after the depiction of Raakkamma and Paakkiaraj's episode, the author briefly describes the miseries of the Dalit women who love and marry against the will of their parents. She depicts the miserable condition of such a woman through an anonymous character. Most of the Dalit women are the victims of their drunkard husbands. Even during pregnancy, the women are mercilessly beaten by their drunkard husbands though theirs is a love marriage. However, because of his drinking habit, he tortures his wife every day and does not give any money to her for family maintenance. Her parents escape from the responsibility of protecting their daughter from domestic violence just by making an excuse that she has herself chosen the bridegroom. Therefore, she herself has to manage to live with him.

In fact, even if it were an arranged marriage, her parents would not do anything except leave their daughter to her so-called fate. It is this miserable plight of the Dalit women that is poignantly reflected in this context. Man has the freedom to spend his earnings as he wishes; his consort cannot question him. This is why women in a family have to bear the burden of family maintenance. If she defies her husband and questions his earnings, she is violently beaten by him.

The discriminative and unequal work division that has long been in existence between man and woman in a traditional family set up in India is reflected in this novel through the characters of Chinnappan and Kaaliamma. No attempts are made by the governments under capitalism to eliminate the unequal domestic work division as the 'domestic socialization' would inevitably lead to the emergence of a demand from the masses for 'production socialization'. In this context, the author analyses the unequal share of work between man and woman through the narrator's words. She comments that though men and women work in the fields and come home exhausted, men go off straight away to the 'bazaar' (market) to pass their time. However, the women have to engage themselves in all household tasks like washing vessels, cleaning the house, collecting water, gathering firewood, going to shops to buy rice and other provisions, cooking food, feeding husband and children, etc. It is only after completing all these chores that they have to eat whatever is leftover and go to bed.

When the narrator reflects on how men suppress their wives, she gets an answer that men 'have to be like dogs with their tails rolled up when they are in the fields and dealing with their landlords.' They have no other way to show their strength in those circumstances, and they show their prowess at home on their wives and children. All their suppressed anger is visited upon the members of their family at home. Though the conditions of all women are the same concerning the aspect of female subjugation in patriarchy, the conditions of Dalit women are worse than those of the upper caste women. Bama shows the difference between the living conditions of upper-caste women and Dalit women.

The upper-caste women need not work in the fields to fill their and their children's bellies. Unlike the Dalit women, they need not undergo physical and mental harassment at the work spot. Nevertheless, they have to lead lives as second-rated human beings in their families. Very often, they, too, are the victims of the wrath of their husbands. Despite their miserable conditions in the family, they never empathise and sympathize with the Dalit women who suffer both in the family and outside.

Further, they 'treat Dalit women with contempt as if they were the creatures of a different species, who have no sense of honour or self–respect.' There is another fact concerning the lives of the upper caste women: they do not have the freedom to move outside their houses, and their lives are confined only to the four walls of their houses. They pass on their time eating and gossiping, depending on their husbands for every trivial thing. In contrast to the living style of the upper caste women, the Dalit women lead independent lives "earning at least a few coins a day". Like the upper caste women, they need not 'hold out their palms to their husbands for every little expense'. However, the Dalit women are treated with contempt not only by the upper caste women but also by the other institutions starting with "police to the priest", who often blame and humiliate the women of the Dalit community. Bama, in this context, advocates that Dalit women take up this challenge as the government, too, has failed to do anything to redress this injustice.

In this context, it is evident that Bama does not look into the existing exploitative social relations in contemporary society for knowing the causes behind gender oppression. Instead, she thinks that the causes for gender oppression are the pessimistic outlook and cowardice of women. "... If we stand up for ourselves without caring whether we die or survive, they'll creep away with their tails between their legs." (p. 66). Comparing the men with onions, she advocates that women rebel against male chauvinism. She says, "As we peel onions, nothing will remain at last". In this context, we should be mindful of the assertion of J.V. Stalin:

> "*Theory becomes purposeless if it is not connected with revolutionary practice, just as practice gropes in the dark if its path is not illumined by revolutionary theory (Stalin. 1954).*"

The mere fight without any revolutionary theory against male chauvinism cannot replace the discriminative gender relations with humane, equal relations between man and woman. The author is not conscious of this historical truth. However, the point she raises on the capability of a woman who can achieve several kinds of tasks in her day-to-day life is worth considering. She challenges men to do the work women usually do in the fields and at the houses. Bama appeals to all women to fight for their rights.

In one of the contexts, Bama is critical of the hypocritical perspective of the upper–caste women. She comments that upper–caste women give the superficial impression that they never quarrel amongst themselves nor with their husbands. Moreover, they criticize that it is only in the streets of Dalits that there are fights and vulgar quarrels all the time. However, Bama reveals the disputes which take place between the upper–caste women and their husbands. She pinpoints that the upper–caste women submit to their husbands bearing domestic violence as they have to depend on their husbands to run the family. However, the Dalit women, unlike upper-caste women, go out to earn. They work on par with men and earn their wages. Though the men spend their wages at liquor shops and hotels, the women look after the houses.

Bama questions the irrational subordination of Dalit women to their husbands. Some women bear the domestic violence silently and suffer a life of hellish torment. "On the one side, she is worn out with physical toil; on the other, she is beaten until she is left with only a half or a quarter-life" (ibid. p. 67). Bama, in this context, opines that the problems of women are associated with the inner quality of boldness. She thinks that women must dare to take control of their lives. However, the issue of women is deeply associated with the existing patriarchy. Patriarchal society is a male-dominated society in which a man is considered an asset to the family. He is the master of the family. While he is regarded as a master, the rest of the family members become either slaves or subordinates. Then the relationship between them is a master-slave or subordinate relationship. That is why a man as a husband unleashes violence on his wife, and as a father, he often resorts to dictatorial excesses.

The patriarchal societies came into existence with the replacement of 'mother right' by the 'father right' in society. While the mother right had been in practice, there was no private property, so there was no gender discrimination. Whenever private property was being established in society, the mother right was begun to be gradually replaced by the father right. This has caused women to undergo such miserable conditions since then. And these gender discriminations and gender oppression will be eliminated in egalitarian societies through cultural revolutions, like the one [though not wholly successful] in the early 70s of the 20th century in the People's Republic of China. But the author, Bama, does not advocate women to be a part of the ongoing socialist movements. She supports that women are to be courageous and to take control of their lives. So long as exploitative production relations exist among people, the dominant exploit and oppress the weak; similarly, in exploitative patriarchal societies, the dominant man exploits and oppresses the vulnerable woman. Ranganayakamma writes:

The relation between men and women is not such a 'class' relation. It is a social relation which is not a class relation. Or, it is a family relation. This unequal relation, however, is a consequence of the emergence of classes in society. Hence, the elimination of inequality between men and women is linked with the elimination of exploitative relations (cited from www.ranganayakamma.org).

However, Bama does not have this consciousness. She considers the problem of women as the problem of the lack of courage. She does not even pay attention to criticising liquor shops' establishments and the contemporary governments that view liquor selling as revenue.

The problem of begetting children has been brought before the readers by the author. Most Dalit women put off birth control operations to prevent them from doing hard work in the fields. If they cannot work hard, they cannot meet the economic needs of their families. That is why they would rather prefer begetting children to opt for sterilization. This pathetic condition of the Dalit women is reflected in this context through Maikkanni's mother's character.

Bama lays bare the exploitative nature of men in Dalits through the characters of Maikkanni and her father. Maikkanni, a little girl who works in a matchbox company, earns and gives her wages to her mother. One day her father waylays her and robs her of her wages. Further, he beats her as she has taken a rupee out her wages and spent it. This episode reflected the innumerable similar incidents that often occur in the lives of Dalits and other depressed communities.

Mental Illness of Dalit Women

It is quite a common phenomenon in the class society that the women in middle and upper-middle-class families as the widows or neglected wives suffer from several mental ailments, one of which is schizophrenia. These mental illnesses generally originate from the age-old and pro-men oppressive customs that dictate the women who estrange themselves from worldly desires. It is due to a lack of love, affection, and companionship; they feel lonely even in the physical presence of the other family members. The well-known feminist writer Anita Desai depicts the miserable condition of a typical woman from the upper-middle-class family background in her novel Cry the Peacock through the character of a woman protagonist who ends her life by committing suicide due to a mental illness caused by the mere negligence of her husband who fails to empathise with her. Sigmund Freud contends that it is due to the ungratified sexual needs, the widows are affected with schizophrenia as they vacillate between religious dogmatism and their biological necessity. The problems of women of this sort are also reflected in this novel.

Bama opines that the Dalit women often undergo mental illness due to the lack of "proper night's peace". The women are deprived of proper night's peace and a cordial family environment after working hard all day as they are to satisfy their husbands' lust whenever they demand it. They never get any rest, and therefore, they vent their irritation by quarrelling with others. Bama conveys this through the narrator's words, who says, "because of this, there occur fights and quarrels in the streets of Dalits". While depicting the frustrated lives of the Dalit women, Bama conveys to her readers the actual cause behind the oddity of the Dalit women. She opines that it is due to sexual dissatisfaction in their own lives, the Dalit women resort to using ugly and obscene words in their quarrels. They compare other women as 'their husbands' whores'. In fact, no woman can tolerate if her husband has a liaison with other women. Bama brings this paradoxical tendency of Dalit women before her readers to reveal that male domination is accepted and asserted even by the women.

Even here, it is the man's maleness and power that takes precedence. A woman's body, mind, feelings, words and deeds, and her entire life are all under his control and domination. And we, too, have accepted what they want us to believe that this is actually the right way, that our happiness lies in being enslaved to men. But if only we were to realize that we too have our self–worth, honour and self–respect, we could manage our own lives in our way (ibid. p. 68).

According to dialectical materialism, the secondary imitates and tries to occupy the position of the primary while the primary persistently tries to keep it off. Similarly, the women, who are positioned as the second-rate citizens in patriarchy, blindly and unconsciously accept and assimilate the male supremacy and thereby, they too imitate the dominant traits of men and adhere to the patriarchal morality. This is why the frustrated women resort to using the men's abusive and vulgar language, entirely centred on debasing womanhood. In this context, we should be mindful of the words of the renowned feminist writer Allan Showalter who contends in her book Feminist Poetics that women must get to invent and use a new pro-woman gender system and vocabulary in their language and writings.

Another reason Bama gives us about women's mental illness is back-breaking work in the fields and at the houses. Because of these rigorous working conditions, they pretend as if devils possessed them. Psychologists explain why this abnormal behaviour is that they pretend to be so to get sympathy and recognition. However, ignoring this fact which is also one of the authentic causes, Bama shows only the cause of strenuous work. She says that in addition to the backbreaking work in the fields and at the houses, the women should take up the responsibility of bringing up children, and they should please their husbands whether they like it or not.

From the moment they wake up, they set to work both in their homes and fields. At home, they are pestered by their husbands and children; in the fields, there is back-breaking work besides the harassment of the landlord. When they come home in the evening, there is no time even to draw breath. And once they have collected water and firewood, cooked a kanji and fed their hungry husband and children, even then, they can't go to bed in peace and sleep until dawn. Night after night, they must give in to their husband's pleasure. Even if a woman's body is wracked with pain, the husband is bothered only with his own satisfaction. Women are overwhelmed and crushed by their own disgust, boredom and exhaustion, because of all this. The stronger ones somehow manage to survive all this. The ones who don't have the mental strength are totally oppressed; they succumb to mental ill-health and act as if they are possessed by pays (ibid. p. 59).

Though men should also work hard in the fields, they have the freedom to 'control their women, rule over them, and find their pleasure'. In this context, Bama suggests that women should be "strong"and not fool themselves that devils have possessed them. They need not embrace fatalism to soother their broken hearts. "She advocates women to strengthen their hearts and bodies to survive in this male-dominated society.

> *"I [the narrator] told myself that we must never allow our minds to be worn out, damaged and broken in the belief that this is our fate. Just as we work hard so long as there is strength in our bodies, so too must we strengthen our hearts and minds to survive (ibid. p. 59)."*

It is, of course, highly essential that the women endeavour to strengthen their "hearts and minds"at least as separate individuals for their mere survival. However, at the same time, they should try to unite and fight against the oppressive patriarchal work division and the other exploitative conventions in an organized manner. Bama fails to permeate such consciousness in Dalit women through her novel.

The Harassment of Woman by Woman

Under feudalism and capitalism, male domination is accepted even by the women who, out of innocence and ignorance, accept the sanctity of the so-called patriarchal morality forced upon them. That is why contradictions arise between a woman and another woman. If any rumour spread about the chastity of a woman, her life becomes hellish. She is harassed with rude comments by the other women themselves. It is this social reality that is reflected in this novel.

Mariamma does not commit any mistake. In fact, when the landlord, Kumarasami Ayya, tries to molest her, she escapes from his sexual assault. However, to defend himself, he calls her caste-elder and cooks up a story that she has a liaison with Manikkam, who belongs to her caste. However, much she condemns those fake allegations, people do not trust her. Significantly, the women make 'insinuating remarks' wherever she goes. Mariamma is entirely fed up with such remarks undergoing mental agony.

Even when she was working out in the fields or on the threshing floor, people would always make insinuating remarks about her having been called up before the village council. Mariamma began to feel totally fed up with life. 'For no fault of mine, I get abused wherever I go. Did I ever look that fellow in the face even? Yet the people of this village call me every kind of name' (ibid. p. 40).

The author, in this context, expresses her annoyance through the words of the narrator, who says that women do not "show any pity or compassion towards other women."

In a class society, internal conflicts or contradictions commonly arise within the working class. They do not know who their real enemy is, and so they quarrel among themselves. Sometimes, those quarrels cost the lives of meek persons like Mariamma. That is why Karl. Marx advocates cultural revolutions after the establishment of a socialist economic base are necessary. According to him, the proletariat could 'get rid of the muck of the ages' only in communist societies through the socialist economic base, the socialist work division and the proletariat cultural revolutions (cited from Ranganayamma's ... Marx is a Must). However, the author's perspective is not one of the communists. So, she does not reach a solution of this kind. She tries to find out a solution to the problem in the individual protest of women. But people like Mariamma cannot rebel against social injustice. They just go with the flow. They embrace fatalism and cannot protest the harassment of their husbands. Quite miserably, their lives are trampled under the iron heel of patriarchy.

Being unable to do anything, she marries Manikkam. Because of the dishonest act of a landlord, her whole life is destroyed. On the one hand, she is harassed by her husband; on the other hand, she is pestered by other women. The narrator also undergoes the harassment of the other women who speak ill of her lifestyle among themselves. They comment when she goes to a 'coffee shop to have a cup of coffee'. When she rents a house on her own and leads an independent life, the other women criticize that 'she is leading a life like a man'. Even her colleagues, too, cannot understand her feelings of self-respect. "Even women teachers who are my colleagues find my lifestyle unbearable. They keep a sharp watch on whatever I do, and spread tales in no time, embroidering and adding whatever they like to imagine" (ibid. p. 121).

So long as the women, who are victimized by the firmly established patriarchal morality, are ignorant of the underlying cause of the harassment of a woman by woman, they can never achieve peace, self-respect and equality on par with men.

The Socio-Religious Chains

Even if the narrator Pathima is a teacher, she too meets with several problems. However, the living conditions of the poor Dalit women are both humiliating and pitiful. They often encounter the upper–caste men's molestations in the fields and the humiliating treatment of the priests at church. In the author's words, they 'must lick the priest's shoes and be his slaves while he threatens them with tales of God, Heaven, and Hell'. When they go to houses, they are to submit themselves to their husbands' torment.

The women are deprived of proper food or drink, but they have to bear the children one after another. During the time of delivery, they are rarely admitted to hospitals, and therefore they should deliver their children at home under the care of country midwives in a makeshift way. Sometimes, many women die during the time of delivery or soon after. It happens because men do not undergo birth control operations, thinking they lose strength if they are operated on. Consequently, the women keep begetting children. Women, too, cannot prefer birth control operations. Because, if they undergo the operation of sterilization, they have to be home for some days during which they cannot work in the fields. Subsequently, their children will have to be starved at home, as the men in their families never bother about all these problems.

Another responsibility of the women is childcare. As the women and their girl children engage in the fields and factories, their tiny babies are not cared for by anyone. "The two and three-year-olds wander about with the street dogs and pigs from morning to night". The author gives this explanation as an answer to the criticism of the so-called civilized society, which often speaks ill of the Dalit children who wander in the streets. Bama, in this context, blames men who never carry their children but go off in the evenings to the shops and the other meeting places. As they return home only to eat and go to sleep, the women are also burdened with childcare work.

Bama discusses the aspect of the imposition of several restrictions on the movement of women. One of those is that women are not allowed to go to the cinema. The reason, which is disclosed through the words of Paatti, is that the presence of the Dalit women might cause the eruption of riots between the upper castes and Dalits. Because she says, 'all sorts of fellows from different castes' would go to the cinema. If any of them misbehaved with the Dalit women, it would lead to conflict, leading to a riot. However, the same may not happen when the upper caste women go to the cinema because no man dares to misbehave.

Bama, in this context, unconsciously discloses the fact that the unequal production relations have been the basis for the occurrence of atrocities on the underprivileged. The author exhibits this truth through the words of the character of Patti. Upper caste people own the lands, and some of them are landlords too. Dalits are just agricultural labourers. If they venture to struggle against the landholding class, they cannot get work (livelihood) in the fields of upper castes. Because of this, Dalits silently bear the atrocities of the landlords on most occasions. To a possible extent, they try to avoid conflict with the upper castes.

Unless the production relations are changed, Dalits cannot be liberated from the atrocities of upper castes. In the words of Paatti, men cannot lay their hands on the upper caste women as they have 'caste – power, and money power'. However, the Dalit women do not have the above two. "Even if a fellow assaults one of us, it's difficult to stand up to him or make an enemy of him. Because in the end, we have to go to him for employment. How long can we keep up the fight?" (ibid. p. 105).

Saying that women should undergo blows and beatings, shame and humiliation, the author feels that at least a little education would make women aware of their problems. However, she does not advocate the struggle against patriarchy, whose organizing principle is economic exploitation. When men humiliate women, she says the women do get furious and frustrated in vain as they suppress their feelings.

There is a depiction of the further problems in the miserable lives of the Dalit women. Bama raises the aspect of lack of education in Dalit women. She tries to bring the general perspective of the people who conceive that mere education would end all problems. Of course, it is true to some extent that at least a little education can undoubtedly sow the seeds of social awakening in the down-trodden. The literacy in the women enable them to know about the world, and this knowledge, in turn, boosts their morale to resist the atrocities of landlords at work spot. The author mentions this fact through the words of the character of Subbamma. However, she ends the conversation between Subbamma and the other women in the same context with a pessimistic conclusion.

"Subbamma said, 'Because we haven't been to school or learnt anything, we go about like slaves all our lives, from the day we are born till the day we die. As if we are blind, even

> *though we have eyes. That is why any old dog will make a grab at us when we are working in the fields. But it's only by struggling like this that we can eat; otherwise, we have to starve, that's all (ibid. p. 118).* "

The problem of Dalits who need to rent houses from others is also discussed in one of the contexts in this novel. Usually, people do not like to rent the vacant portions of their houses to Dalits who are not in a position to build their own houses. Even if they decide to hide their caste, they cannot keep it hidden for a long time. The author, in this connection, expresses her anguish and raises the question, why Dalits, in fact, should hide their identity.

I am a paraichi; yes I am a paraichi. And I don't like to hide my identity and pretend I belong to a different caste. The question beats away in my mind: why should I tell a lie and live a false life? Women of other castes don't face this problem. They can move where they choose, take a house, set up a livelihood. But we are denied the basic right to pay our money and rent a house. Are we so despicable to these others? (ibid. p. 121).

Apart from the problem of renting houses, the author raises the issues of the Dalit women who want to live by themselves. If a woman lives alone, people generally assume that she is a 'prostitute'. The author criticizes the rotten minds of the people who consider that a married woman is a man's property; if she is unmarried, she is regarded as the common property of many fellows. She questions the unjustifiable assumption that is powerfully prevalent in the contemporary male-dominated society in this regard. She asks why a woman should belong to anyone at all and why she cannot live by herself.

A Contrast Between the Living Conditions of the Upper Caste Women and the Dalit Women

The women in the upper castes are constrained to move out of the houses. They are not even allowed to work in the fields. In fact, they do not need to do so as all the necessary provisions are supplied by their men. Therefore, they 'stay shut up within four walls, all twenty – four hours of the day" (Bama. p. 66). The author, in this context, draws a contrast between the living conditions of the upper caste women and those of the Dalit women. She says in this regard that the Dalit women at least have the freedom of moving outside their houses; they work in the fields and earn money and run their families, but the upper caste women always confine themselves within four walls. According to the author, the Dalit women have the courage and freedom to question the atrocious behaviour of their husbands as it is the women (in the Dalit communities) who look after their families with their wages. However, the upper caste women silently bear the domestic violence and cannot question their husbands' unjustifiable dominance; they entirely submit themselves to their husbands.

The author exposes the widow problem also in the upper castes and Dalits. If a girl loses her husband, i.e. if her husband dies, the girl is made a widow in the upper castes, and thereafter, several restrictions are imposed upon her. She is not to attend 'good occasions' and is not even allowed to wear flowers, use bindi and turmeric ever again; she is mercilessly thrown into a corner of the house. On the contrary, if a girl's husband dies, she can remarry again in the Dalit communities. She is allowed to attend the auspicious occasions and mingles with the other women. She does not need to sit in a corner. This is a positive and progressive cultural aspect in the Dalit castes. Contrary to this, widows are not honoured in the upper castes and even given enough food.

Bama draws a contrast between the upper caste women and the Dalit women in several other aspects too. In chapter twelve, she explains the poor economic conditions of the Dalit women who live in small huts wherein they would have to cook and sleep. They do not possess individual bathrooms, and therefore they cannot bath at their home. So, they usually have their baths in the wells in the fields of landlords. Bama views this poor condition of the Dalit women as something else that facilitates them to have the freedom of swimming while the upper caste women are restricted from coming out of their houses. This miserable condition of the Dalit women reflects the poverty that has deprived of them the basic amenities. As the upper caste women have bathrooms in their houses themselves, they, of course, don't need to go out for a bath.

The Freedom of Remarriage

The freedom of remarriage is customary in Dalits and the other lower castes. The women remarry if their husbands die or when they cannot continue to live with their husbands. However, this freedom is not found in Christianity. The Dalit Christian converts whose husbands leave cannot remarry according to the Christian religious code as the Christian ethical code asserts that the marriage between a man and a woman is held to the accord of God. So man [a human being] has no right to break that bond. This is why they cannot leave their husbands, terminating their marriages, even if they are subject to domestic violence and harassment. This cultural aspect in Dalit Christians is further discussed in the forthcoming paragraph in this chapter itself.

The tradition of remarriage is in practice in Dalit Hindus. The author upholds this convention through the character of Pecchi. The husband of Pecchi is a drunkard who doesn't give any money for the household expenses. Furthermore, he beats her up every day and snatches away all her earnings. Unable to endure her husband's cruelty, she goes back to her father's house and asks her father to talk to the caste elder to arrange separation. The caste elder calls a meeting of the panchayat and ends the marriage. Later Pecchi remarries another man and begets a child too.

Bama highlights the progressive aspect in the culture of the downtrodden. What the upper–caste women could not even think of is a reality in the lives of the Dalit women. Because, if an upper-caste woman leaves her husband and chooses to live alone, people will keep on perturbing her, and sometimes they may 'even drive her to her death.'

The culture of the upper–castes is of the Brahmanist one. In Brahmanism, the woman has no respectable place. She is considered a second-rated being according to the religious scriptures. Aristotle said the female is female by virtue of a certain lack of qualities. Saint Thomas called a woman an imperfect man and so an incidental being. In Genesis, the woman (Eve) is depicted as being made from a supernumerary bone of man (Adam). Sigmund Freud says that female sexuality is shaped by envy. While several thinkers support and propagate female subordination, Karl Marx declares all human beings are equal. Influenced by Marx's writings, Simone de Beauvoir argues in her book The Second Sex :

> *""Man's dominance has been secured through the ages by an ideological power, legislators, priests, scientists and philosophers have all promoted the idea of woman's subordination". "*

Chalam, a renowned Telugu feminist – writer and critic, says that like man, 'woman, too, has body, brain and heart and therefore she needs exercise to her body, knowledge to brain and experience to heart'.

The woman has been an unequal partner in the traditional family setup. In every aspect, she is made inferior to a man, i.e. to her father, brother and husband. Beatings and other forms of physical violence are common modes of oppression of women by men. Woman's meaningless endurance of domestic violence in silence is hailed as a virtue in epics.

In Marxist understanding, gender inequalities are a part of class inequalities, so gender oppression is part and parcel of class oppression. As gender oppression and religious dogmatism are not a hindrance to capital accumulation, the capitalists never evince interest in eliminating gender discrimination and oppression from society. Moreover, they try to encash both social maladies. The root cause of gender oppression lies in the existing exploitative production system. Unless the proletariat that constitutes both the men and the women liberates themselves from the existing exploitative production relations, the genuine endeavours of the progressive forces for the establishment of gender equality cannot be fruitful. Nevertheless, women's organized and unorganized struggles for gender equality can be continued unhesitatingly even under capitalism.

The emancipation of women becomes possible only by replacing the exploitative production system with a non – exploitative production system. The dialectical and historical materialism asserts that nothing exists in absolute independence as everything is interdependent. Therefore, class oppression and gender oppression are also interdependent. The latter has emerged as an inevitable consequence of the former. Thus, while the women struggle against the patriarchal injustices, they should fight against the root cause of their problems in their daily lives. Unless they have an ultimate aim of changing the exploitative production system, their current struggles --however much valiant they are-- will never bear fruit. However, Bama lacks this consciousness and projects gender oppression in isolation, making no connection with class oppression and class struggle.

Though Brahmanism creeps in several aspects of social life in Dalits, they still keep their own culture in their social life. That is why it has become possible for Dalit women to liberate themselves from the chains of their husbands' harassment and remarry again. Still, the aspect of remarriage remains a mere dream for the women of the upper castes. It is this difference that is reflected in this novel.

But it seemed to me that it was a very good thing that some of our women had the option of ending their marriages. Because it meant a woman need not spend her entire life, burning and dying, with a man she dislikes, just because of this thing called marriage. But I also felt sad that Christian women didn't have this chance; on the other hand, many upper-caste women could not even think do it in their wildest dreams (Bama. p. 93).

Bama, in another context, reveals the difficulties of the Dalit women who end their marriages. It is not a big deal for men to end the marriage and remarry, but it is a great ordeal for women. On most occasions, it is the man who ends the marriage and marries another. So this tradition in the oppressed class actually damages the women even though it facilitates their escape from their husbands' torture.

Aside from the religious restrictions, caste restrictions are imposed on women in the paraiyar community. The pallar and chakkiliyaar castes women can end their marriages and come back to their parents' houses. They can lead lives working in the fields or somewhere. However, the case is different with paraiyar women. Being unable to bear the torture, if a girl leaves her husband and returns to her parent's house, she is usually compelled to return to her husband. Because the caste elders reprimand her parents and advise them to force their daughter to live with her husband, even if her husband is cruel to her. In this context, Bama sneers at the tyrannical tendency and male chauvinism of the caste elders. Bama writes:

Among the paraiyar, there's a different way of settling it. Say a girl can't stand her husband and comes away, leaving him. Do you think our community will leave her alone? There's no way she can live by herself, go to work, and earn her livelihood. They'll call a panchayat meeting, hold a trial and force the girl to go back. And who do they call to the trial? They never even summon the girl. They call her father or her brother and finish it off by ordering him,

> *""Give the girl a couple of slaps and tell her she must go and live with her husband. And these are our village elders!"* (ibid. p. 96)."*

Bama, in this context, discusses the problems of the Dalit Hindus. Owing to the custom of remarriage in the Dalit Hindus, the man can quickly leave his wife and remarry another woman, but it cannot be easier for the woman to remarry another man. Therefore, the Dalit Hindu women are "both blessed and cursed". In Bama's opinion, religion also could not protect the interests of women, especially the Dalit women. The Dalit Christians cannot leave their husbands by ending their marriage because it is, in principle, against God.

At the time of marriage, a Dalit Christian woman makes a 'solemn promise' that she will live with the man she marries, "in sickness and in health, for better for worse, for richer for poorer". The priest blesses the couple, saying that no law, panchayat, or courts of justice can separate the married couple. Hence, the Dalit Christian women have no scope to end their marriages. Once married, they have to live with their husbands till the doomsday according to the promise they make in front of the priest. In fact, the custom of remarriage is undoubtedly a boon, as a woman can survive in society living by herself but cannot be happy even for a moment living with an unkind, cruel husband. So, indisputably the custom of remarriage is a boon and therefore a progressive aspect in the culture. The sheer experiential outlook of the author by ignoring the intrinsic interconnectivity of such happenings made her opine that the custom of remarriage is "both a boon and a curse".

The Dalit Christian women are discriminated against even at the church. They are to clean the church and its surroundings; they, in return, can get the blessings of God. The priest never entrusts this job to the upper–caste Christian women. The law of dialectical and historical materialism asserts that economics determine the nature of existing social (production) relations among the people. If in principle, the upper castes were not of the propertied class, the priests would not give them such a privilege. Bama ridicules this hypocrisy of priests with her sarcastic comment that whether the upper caste Christian women do not need the blessings of God as they simply stand to one side when the Dalit women clean the church. Bama conveys this discrimination to her readers in the words of the narrator:

> "...and then march in grandly and sit down before anyone else. I've stood it as long as I could, and at last, I went and complained to the nuns. And do you know what they said? It seems we will gain merit by sweeping the church and that God will bless us specially. See how they fool us in the name of God! Why, don't those people need God's blessings too?

(ibid. p. 119)."

Bama makes it clear, in this context, that the lack of education in Dalits is not the real reason for their failure to get respect from other castes. In fact, she argues that the little education the Dalit women receive in no way helps them in their lives. She writes, "... But it seems what they teach is really of no use to us. Our lessons go one way, our lives go another way. There's really no connection at all between the two" (ibid. p. 119).

Bama explores and exposes the endless problems that the Dalit women undergo in their daily lives in this novel. The discriminative outlook of the people in the patriarchal society and the harassment of male chauvinists at the workplace and home manifest in a class society. Furthermore, women in general also absorb the patriarchal dominative tendencies and become isolated even under capitalism. All these social maladies are reflected in this novel. Cinzia Aruzza aptly says:

"Gender oppression and racial oppression do not correspond to two autonomous systems which have their own particular causes; they have become an integral part of capitalist society through a long historical process that has dissolved preceding forms of social life"(Aruzza. 2014).

Gender oppression though not originated under capitalism, it has become an integral part and one of the means by which it can continue its saga of capital accumulation.

CHAPTER SEVEN

Four Novels: An Assessment And Proposition

Some similar and a few distinct aspects are found in all these four novels. As these novels depict the problems of Dalits, it is quite natural that all these novels essentially have some similar features. Although some similarities are there in the themes of the novels, there are differences in the authors' perspectives who put forth the problems of Dalits from their respective outlooks. Even though there are differences in their perspectives, the problems of Dalits were objectively reflected in their novels. Out of the four authors, three are Dalits, and the remaining one is a non – Dalit. While P. Sivakami, the author of The Grip of Change, G.Kalyana Rao, the author of Untouchable Spring, Bama, the author of Sangati (Events) are Dalits, Mulk Raj Anand, the author of Untouchable, is a non – Dalit. All these four novels are the debut novels of the writers. It can be conceived that the genre of the novel is potent to comprehensively reflect human life or a part of it in complex social phenomena. However, the novels of identity that are themed around a particular issue representing a specific section of people are restricted by themselves, unable to portray the characteristics of several other social institutions. This is why the generous upper-caste character like Ramireddy in Untouchable Spring has not been developed as significant characters though they deserve to be so.

As the scope of the novel, Untouchable is limited only to depict the problems of an outcast youth, the characters with generosity, Havaldar Charat Sing and Hakim Bhagawan Das have not been developed to major characters. Similarly, no male character has been projected as heroic in Sangati, while no upper-caste character is found noble and generous in The Grip of Change.

Except for Bakha in Untouchable, the protagonists in all these three novels appear as progressive forces as they either work or think for the transformation of society. Bakha, too, thinks of liberation only from his inhuman latrine cleaning job. Still, nonetheless unlike Immanuel, Jessy, Chandran, Gowry and Pathima (the narrator in Sangati), Bakha is not aware of the necessity of changing the unequal social relations in society. In Untouchable Spring, Immanuel and Jessy join the revolutionary party, potent to abolish the oppressive and exploitative social relations in society. In The Grip of Change, Chandran tries to unite his co-workers who work in his and the other companies located nearby. Fathima being a rebel at heart, observes, contemplates and raises several questions concerning a woman predicament. Though there are differences in the consciousnesses of the protagonists, all of them aspire for progressive change in the lives of the depressed.

The problems of self–respect, oppression and gender oppression are the most common similar features in all these novels. In Untouchable Spring, Yellanna encounters the issue of self–respect when the upper caste elders oppose the newly formed proceedings of the performance. When the upper caste elders order him to stop calling on pedamala and pedamadiga before the performance, Yellanna and Naganna, having felt oppressed, decide to abandon their performance. They understand that they are deprived of the right to honour themselves. When they themselves cannot honour their elders, they feel it is meaningless to give performances. Contemplating this issue, Yellanna leaves home with an indefinite aim while the only question of self–respect reverberates in his mind. After leaving home, he becomes a folklorist and song weaver and whereby he freely weaves and sings songs in front of his people.

He sings in the fields and before the coolies, so now none can raise an objection to his performances. One can infer from this act that Yellanna becomes mala bairagi through his unconscious efforts, and thereby he could regain self–respect as an incognito individual artist. As Yellanna, he is prevented from performing in the village, but as a mala bairagi, he cannot be prevented from singing before people. Craving such freedom to unlock his heart to console himself, Yellanna leaves home. However, he has no definite aim and specific plan of action for bringing in better change in the miserable living conditions of his fellow Dalits.

Under feudalism, the underprivileged cannot live with self-respect. G. Kalyana Rao conveys this truth by depicting several other incidents like the dead bullock incident, entry of Vishnu temple, lake water incident and so on. He depicts how the oppressive and exploitative forces harass the marginalized who invite progressive change in their lives. This social reality is reflected when Dalits decide to refrain from eating the meat of dead cattle. Laying bare the exploitative and oppressive social relations through the dead bullock incident, the author shows how Dalits are forcibly and cruelly made to eat the meat of dead cattle when they consider their abstinence from the flesh of dead cattle would fetch them self–respect.

The selfish motive of the feudal lords who try to befriend Dalits in the guise of pseudo-social organizations like Harijan Seva Sanghs is revealed through the episode of temple entry and the subsequent purificatory ritual. He also revealed the hypocritical nexus between the landlords and Gandhiji. Kalyana Rao tells us through the words of the character Ramanujam that the Harijan Seva Sangh aims only to protect the Hindu religion from mass religious conversions but not to eradicate untouchability.

Being a communist revolutionary writer, Kalyana Rao asserts the necessity of joining the revolutionary communist party for the depressed to liberate themselves from exploitation, oppression, and social discrimination. In this novel, Reuben, Immanuel and Jessy are communists. Immanuel, the son of Reuben, dies in an encounter during the Srikakulam peasants movement led by Naxalites. Jessy, the son of Immanuel, joins the Communist Party of India - Marxist and Leninist (People's War). Here, Kalyana Rao comments that joining a revolutionary party is not an ideal for Dalits but a necessity. We can infer from these lines that Dalits can emancipate themselves from the pangs of untouchability only through the proletariat cultural revolution, which could only occur after a successful political revolution. This is why, Kalyana Rao says, revolution is not an ideal for Dalits but a necessity. From the above discourse, it can be stated that Untouchable Spring is a revolutionary novel with socialist realism.

While Kalyana Rao's is of a communist revolutionary perspective, P. Sivakami's outlook is of parliamentary democratic perspective with a shade of feminism. In her The Grip of Change, the protagonist Kathamuthu is a parliamentary democratic political leader. Though this character is put to criticism sometimes, his ways to settle the disputes between Dalits and upper caste lords are implicitly appreciated by the author. When Tangam is beaten, and when the huts of Dalits are burnt, he demands money as compensation. In fact, it is the idea of the author herself. Sivakami shows Kathamuthu's character as the one who suppresses his wives at home, and ridicules the practice of polygamy and patriarchal dominative nature of the men in the Dalit communities.

Chandran and Gowri, too, work within the frame of parliamentary democracy. Gowri receives a doctorate and assists her cousin Chandran in his trade union activities. Chandran tries to unite the Dalit workers with the other workers who belong to the other depressed castes, amicably mingling with them. Here, Sivakami's idea --the unity of depressed castes is the unity of workers-- is reflected in her depiction of Chandran's trade union activities. Chandran's efforts seem to have been in congruence with the wake-up call of Karl Marx, "The workers of the world, unite!", nevertheless, so long as the workers do not try to get rid of caste consciousness, or at least they try to acquire working class consciousness and place it over the caste consciousness, they cannot establish socialism only under which the socio-economic and political inequalities are eliminated.

The characterization of Chandran and Gowri reveals the fact that the author P. Sivakami seems to have been influenced by the ideology of Kanshi Ram, the founder president of the Bahujan Samaj Party, which had its foundations in the parliamentary democratic principles. However, the egalitarian society cannot be established in the pro bourgeois political system in which the propertied class rule the country. At the same time, the poor, that mainly and majorly constitute Dalits and the other weaker sections, always remain ruled. The rule by the propertied class, which has possessed all the resources in its hand, cannot let the depressed live in peace and self-respect. When any disputes occur between the dominant and the depressed classes, the state machinery stands by the dominant class's side. This fact is depicted in Untouchable Spring and The Grip of Change.

In Untouchable, though being sweepers, Bakha craves self–respect, and Sohini does not yield to the sexual desire and demand of pundit Kalinath. Bakha believes that his sweeping work deprives him of self–respect. So, he comes to a resolution that the latrine cleaning machine will fetch him self-respect liberating him from all humiliations in the future. In Sangati, Pathima also encounters the problem of self-respect. Still, miserably, she faces this problem from her fellow women who unduly comments on her chosen lifestyle, i.e., self-reliant living.

Another common feature in these four novels is oppression which is cultural, economic, political and gender-related. In Untouchable Spring, the village elders dictate Yellanna and Naganna not to invite pedamala and pedamadiga. When Dalits refrain from eating the meat of a dead bullock, the village elders torture them and make them eat. Dalits are subject to indiscriminate oppression in the Valasapadu land dispute. When they acquire lands, the upper caste landlords resort to violence on them. In this violent attack, besides Martin, several other Dalits are killed. Feudal forces become intolerant when they are to lose their hegemonic control over their ill-gotten property. In any incident, if the depressed communities happen to get even a tiny tenement of land, they are harassed and subject to violence which is unleashed in several forms. The possession of land by Dalits makes them self-reliant, which in turn fetches them self-respect. When Dalits try to live with self–respect, they are often subject to violence with impunity. This social reality is reflected in the episode of the Valasapadu land issue in Untouchable Spring.

Through the Avalapadu lake water incident, Kalyana Rao depicts how state machinery unleashes violence on the oppressed. Though suffered at the hands of upper-caste lords and the police personnel, Dalits, at last, attain equal right over the lake water. They can get down the lake and have water, though some need to attend court adjournments. This shows the author's optimism and faith in social movements to attain equal rights over public utilities. However, in Untouchable, M.R. Anand leaves this social malady of Dalits with a mere description of the pathetic living conditions of 'untouchables'. As the stories of the novels Untouchable Spring (the story which runs from Yellanna to Reuben) and Untouchable set up in the then existing feudal societies, it has become inevitable for the writers to discuss the then burning problem of Dalits --the deprivation of the right to get access to public utilities. This is the reason why this problem is reflected in both novels.

In contrast, in the other two novels, The Grip of Change and Sangati, whose stories are set up in the 1970s and 1980s, and in the 1990s, this problem of Dalits --the deprivation of the right to get access to public utilities-- is not reflected. Because the production relations originated from the capitalist mode of a production system were gradually pushing away the old feudal production relations in which religious dogmatism dictates the social life of people. That is why Karl Marx comments that it is not possible for the writers to create a character like 'Achilles' after the invention of the gun.

Sivakami, too, describes oppression on the depressed and dispossessed by the dominant through the characters of Thangam and Kamalam. As Paranjothy Udayar forcibly keeps Thangam, his wife Kamalam gets Thangam thrashed by her brothers and brother-in-law. Yet another aspect that Sivakami skillfully deals with is gender oppression in the families of Dalit leaders. Kathamuthu, though he works for the people of his community, oppresses his two wives. Both class oppression and gender oppression are depicted in The Grip of Change. While the class oppression is shown through the characters of Paranjyothi Udayar and Tangam, the upper caste landlords and Dalits in cheri, the gender oppression is exposed through the characterization of Kathamuthu and his two wives Nagamani and Kanagavalli.

The orthodox Hindu social structure oppresses Bakha in Untouchable. Unlike his father, a fatalist, Bakha thinks of a way out from the humiliations and oppression. He feels like retaliating when he is slapped by the "touched man" in the market. Mulk Raj Anand treats the character of Bakha as a representative of the depressed castes in the modern age. Being optimistic about the future is one of the characteristics of the modern age. He who wrote this novel with the perspective of humanism empathizes and sympathizes with the untouchables of the day.

While the oppression of Dalits by the upper castes is the theme in Untouchable and Untouchable Spring, gender oppression is the major theme in Sangati (Events) and The Grip of Change. Bama's outlook is one of the feminists. While she only focuses on the problems of the Dalit women, Mulk Raj Anand and G. Kalyana Rao bring before various issues of Dalits. In order to expose how the lives of Dalit women are crushed and crippled at the hands of their husbands and their fathers, Bama has created the character of Mariamma. In fact, Bama creates every character to explain to her readers the gender oppression within the Dalit community. Bama says that the Dalit women are doubly marginalized: first being a woman, and second, being a person who belongs to the lowest community, i.e. Avarnas [outcasts]. So, the Dalit women are doubly marginalized and doubly oppressed.

However, the author who has brought before us the domestic violence in which the woman, while being young, is oppressed by her father, and by her husband, after the beginning of her marital life, fails to see the prevalence of the 'superior dictates inferior' tendency even among women. She has not touched the aspect of violence -- physical and mental— being unleashed on a daughter–in–law by her mother–in–law in a typical Indian family. Here, the author's fragmented perception of social reality has become a hindrance that has prevented her from looking into the problem of gender oppression which has become an integral part of the 'capitalist power relations'. She has not been aware that domination is the by-product of the exploitative production system. This dominative attribute is absorbed even by the marginalized sections of people in a class society.

Consequently, the causes for the pathetic subaltern status of the women have not come for discussion in this novel. However, the author narrates the innumerable problems that the women, especially the Dalit women, encounter in their day to day lives. Bama has written Sangati with a Dalit feminist outlook.

Several philosophers, thinkers and writers have contributed to the feminist movements. Mary Wollstonecraft's Vindication of Rights of Women (1792), Simone de Beauvoir's The Second Sex (1949), Virginia Woolf's A Room of One's Own, Kate Millet's Sexual Politics, Friedrich Engels's The Origin of The Family (1884), John Stuart Mill's The Subjection of Women (1869) etc., are the significant writings which advocate the liberation of women from gender oppression. Karl Marx and Frederic Engels --as young Hegelians-- also briefly discussed women's predicament in their philosophical work The Holy Family (1844).

Friedrich Engels says that woman enslavement started with the advent of private property in society. Man (the male) being engaged in the production system held all the productive forces such as land, production tools etc., under his control, whereas women who had to be home looking after children and household tasks became dependent on men and inferior to men. Man's hegemony replaced the gender equality prevalent in primitive communism in the patriarchal feudal societies, and thereafter the female subjugation has been in practice. This female subordination is eliminated only in the classless society.

However, Bama ignores the necessity of exploration of the root cause for women predicament. Of course, one need not expect her to do so. She discusses the problems of all Dalit women but tries to find a solution in an isolated individual struggle which is quite an impracticable approach. She advocates that Dalit women should realize their capability of revolting against patriarchy. In a sophomoric manner, she tries to motivate them to stand against patriarchal dominance. Patriarchy is one of the manifestations of class society. If the Dalit women fight against gender and caste discrimination in isolation, they can never attain their emancipation from gender and caste oppression. In Marxist understanding, the Dalit movements and the Dalit feminist movements (in fact, every justifiable movement of identity) are a part of the socialist movement. So they should march on along with the contemporary class struggles which G. Kalyana Rao advocates in his Untouchable Spring.

The aspect of religious conversions is also brought before us in Untouchable Spring, Untouchable and Sangati. The authors of these novels have declared that the religious conversions of Dalits also have failed to fetch them equal social status on par with the caste Hindus. While the deprivation of Dalits' right to access to public utilities is brought before us in Untouchable Spring and Untouchable, the victimization of Dalits by state violence is depicted in The Grip of Change and Untouchable Spring. While the woman's predicament in patriarchy is mirrored in Sangati and The Grip of Change, gender oppression is entirely evaded in Untouchable and Untouchable Spring.

These four novels reflect the problems of Dalits who have been subject to social discrimination and economic exploitation by society's deep rooted oppressive and exploitative institutions. They forthrightly lay bare the shady side of the Indian discriminative social matrix. The unjustifiable hierarchy structure of the power and oppression at various levels and the avoidance of grave socio-economic aspects by religion in the casteist and class-ridden society have been uncovered in these novels.

The major characters in these novels are mainly the oppressed and the oppressors. While the oppressive characters are younger karanam, Atchireddy, Bukkireddy, Chettodu in Untouchable Spring; Paranjothy Udayar and Kathamuthu in The Grip of Change; Pundit Kalinath and the 'touched man' in Untouchable and Kumarasami Ayya, Maanikkam etc., in Sangati, the oppressed characters are Yellanna, Naganna, Simon, Martin, Thangam, Kanagavalli, Nagamani, Bakha, Sohini, Mariyamma and so on. As Reuben, Immanuel and Jessy are communists; they quite naturally question the atrocious nature of the dominant class. All the oppressed characters in these novels suffer humiliation, privation, discrimination and violence.

The exploitation and oppression (economic and social) of one class of society by the other is reflected in all these novels. However, except for G. Kalyana Rao, the remaining three authors turn a blind eye to the discussion of the production relations that have been the basis for caste discriminations, gender oppression and the exploitation of man by man. The history of a society is the history of its production relations at a certain age. Therefore the changing of production relations is to the changing of the history of a particular society in a specific period. These three authors express a passionate desire that the oppression of the underprivileged should vanish from society. Still, they do not advocate the class struggles by which a humane production system will replace the existing production system that is the base of society. They do not conceive that the changes in the production system will eventually lead to changes in the production relations. Though the authors indubitably aspire that the contradictions among the relations of people who belong to various castes and classes should be wiped out, their paths to establish such an ideal society are distinct and different.

While Untouchable Spring is a novel of socialist realism, which, apart from mirroring the social life of people, aims to bring in progressive change in society, the remaining three novels are of social realism, which depicts the society and social events with realism. As G. Kalyana Rao has written his novel with the socialist revolutionary outlook, he has shown that Jessy and Ruby joined a communist revolutionary party at the end. Sivakami embraces the ideology of Kanshi Ram and the Bahujan Samaj Party and offers the parliamentary democratic political approach as a solution to all caste discriminations and oppression in society. Mulk Raj Anand, who puts forth several ideas before Bakha to liberate himself from the curse of untouchability, ultimately gets inclined towards the technological solution, which has proved to be an illusion. Because, even after the induction of the flush system, the evil practice of untouchability is not eradicated in India. Lastly, Though Bama exposes the troubles and tribulations of the Dalit women, she fails to bring before the question of the economic exploitation which forms the basis for gender and racial discrimination.

G. Kalyana Rao has successfully sensitised us about the past - history, and he has brought the present history to our mind. So naturally, there is a scope for us to have dialectical imagination of future history. Yellanna, Chandrayya, Naganna, Reuben, Immanuel, Jessy, Ruby, Gowry, Chandran, and Patheema long for liberty from caste discriminations and oppression while Bakha aspires to liberate himself from scavenging work.

It seems that an attempt to avoid the confrontation with the socialist reality is made by Mulk Raj Anand, P. Sivakami and Bama, in whose novels the justifiable discussion of the production system of the day remains untouched. The tribulations of the oppressed, condemned in these novels, are all the inevitable consequences of the then-contemporary profit-oriented production system whose only aim is to accumulate infinite wealth by a few individuals. However, the authors have viewed and projected these problems of the oppressed as the ones that surface in society due to the influence of the aspects of the superstructure such as caste, religion, culture, ethics, etc., and whereby they abandon the production system untouched. It is the production system on which the superstructure is established. While, except Bama, the authors of Untouchable Spring and The Grip of Change who have risen to the occasion with their chosen ideologies, M.R. Anand who though in the later years manifested himself as a Marxist in his writings [of course, he never admitted that he was a Marxist] could not show any practical solution to the stigmatization to which Dalits are subject to in every sphere of social life.

About Marxism and Ambedkar's Views

In his The Annihilation of Caste, B.R. Ambedkar writes that the attempts to eliminate economic inequalities are to be preceded by the attempts to eliminate social inequalities. Here it seems that B.R. Ambedkar, in principle, denies the primacy of the Marxian understanding and goal, which assert that the basis for all unequal social relations is the exploitative economic base and, therefore, it needs to be changed to eliminate all inhuman and regressive elements that penetrated and permeated the superstructure. Marxism asserts that all the inequalities among people would be eliminated under communism. "Socialist economic base, socialist work division, and the proletarian cultural revolutions are mandatory" for eliminating socio [including caste, gender, racial, etc.] and economic and political inequalities (Ranganayakamma). Though, Ambedkar argued that the progressive struggles should be aimed first at annihilating social inequalities, he proposed "state socialism" whose ideals echoed the Marxist socialist ideals. He also considered "Reservations" for the depressed castes in the spheres of education and employment one of the tools that can bring in progressive change in the economic status of the marginalized. His idea behind the provision of Reservations to the depressed castes is that the bettered economic conditions of Dalits would fetch them a better social status in society. By this, we can clearly see that there is no irreconcilable contradiction between Marxism and Ambedkarism as the latter also has seen a solution to Dalits' problem in the economic sphere.

According to Marx, every society, including the Indian society, survives on three activities: Production, Distribution and Social

Reproduction while caste, religion, race etc., remain as the mere vestigial organs (just as the human beings can continue to live even after the appendectomy surgery) without which the survival and progress of the society can never be hampered. Hence, the base of society is economics, and it is this base that needs to be changed humanely in order to resolve the socio-cultural marginality of Dalits and other depressed castes. In this context, it is apt for us to refer to the opinion of B.R. Ambedkar, who viewed the caste system as 'an exploitative device based on economic interest and the use of force which ultimately leads to caste hegemony, marginalization and unequal distribution of resources amongst the citizens of the same nation'. Here, we should also be mindful of the theory of Daniel Kergoat on the 'consubstantiality' of patriarchal, racial and class relations:

"These are three systems of relations based on exploitation and domination which intersect and are of the same substance (exploitation and domination), while being distinct, like the three persons of the Holy Trinity"(cited from the article "Gender and Capitalism: Debating Cinzia Aruzza's 'Remarks on Gender", viewpoint magazine, 2 Sep. 2014. www.viewpointmag.com)

Not that Dalits belong to the aliened religions, they are segregated from the mainstream of society but as people of a distinct race, they are estranged from society in India. So, the racial discrimination they are being subjected to is based upon economic exploitation, while religious dogmatism, a peripheral aspect of superstructure, is instrumental.

In fact, B.R. Ambedkar has never had hatred of Marxism. Telakapalli Ravi, the writer and literary critic, writes, "Govind Panansare, who was killed by the religious fanatics, mentioned that B.R. Ambedkar expressed his opinion in desperation in the presence of his friend Gaekwad that it was likely that he would join the Communist Party as the Buddhism to which he, along with thousands of Dalits got converted, did not bring in any desired outcome"("Mahada Prasthanam", Andhrajyothi, The Daily News Paper, dated 22 May 2016, print.). Furthermore, there is video graphic evidence that B.R. Ambedkar endorsed Communism. He mentioned in his interview with a BBC journalist that the parliamentary democracy would not be successful in India; it would be replaced with a system like Communism" (His interview with the BBC). The writers like Namdev Dhasal, Babu Rao Bagul etc., who were inspired by the writings and movements of B.R. Ambedkar, have inclined towards Marxism. They envisaged a possible solution to the Dalit issue. However, except for G. Kalyana Rao, the remaining three writers have not shown the cause and effect relationship between the semi-feudal, bourgeois production system and the production relations in contemporary society.

Literature should impel people to face and fight the repression valiantly. Karl Marx and Frederic Engels in The Manifesto of Communist Party say that 'the philosophers have only interpreted the world, in various ways; the point is, however, to change it'. Consciously or unconsciously, every writer supports or advocates or propagandizes a particular school of thought. Therefore, they cannot restrict themselves to the status of a mere recorder of social events. Those who get convinced that the art is not for the sake of art, but the well-being and progress of people essentially believe that the writers have an ethical responsibility to write for motivating and mobilizing people to fight oppression and exploitation.

Varavara Rao, the eminent revolutionary poet and Marxist literary critic, says that when we read either history or fiction, it should propel us to create a new history and instill confidence in us that we shall have our own history and culture in the near future. Furthermore, he says that unless the literature that depicts the struggle in the inner- nuances and dark angles puts forth an optimistic future, at least as a spark in the lightening into the aspirations of society, the fiction has nothing to do with the physical reality in man's social life. The attempts of Jessy and, to some extent, the efforts of Chandran make us optimistic though their world outlooks and chosen paths are different. However, the ideas of Bakha and Pathima do not create any strong impression on our minds. Though not pessimistic, they do not convince us that socio-economic discrimination will vanish in the near future. In order to materialize the dream of B. R. Ambedkar, the valiant fighter for the emancipation of Dalits, the writers who write for the Dalit cause need to write with the aim of making the principle of 'one man - one vote and one man - one value', a day to day reality.

The mere description of the miseries of the oppressed is not enough to achieve and establish a justifiable society. The relationship between those miseries and the then-contemporary production system is to be exposed. It is the prime responsibility of the writers [who wish to establish a justifiable society in place of the unjustifiable one] that they ought to mention at least in an implicit manner in their writings what the oppressed should do for the emancipation from their bondage of oppression and exploitation. All the writers of these novels express their disgust at the cowardice and senseless silence of the victims of the contemporary oppressive institutions. Except for Kalyana Rao, nobody shows them a viable solution to their problems. G. Kalyana Rao, being a revolutionary writer, advocates the importance of intensifying class - struggle as a means for the depressed to liberate themselves from discrimination, exploitation and oppression.

Karl Marx asserted that he had learned significantly about the production relations of past societies through the writings of Homer, Virgil, Shakespeare, Goethe, Dante, Balzac, etc. The class struggles of the slaves under the heroic leadership of Spartacus against the then-Roman imperialists; the strenuous efforts of Changhiz Khan in uniting all the tribes of Mongolian land and thereby transforming them into an invulnerable force against the then monarchical Chinese mighty armies; the socio-economic problems of Gonds [the tribal people who are found in the South Indian forests] and their resultant rebellion under the courageous leadership of Komaram Bheem are brought to light as not that they had been recorded partly by the historians but because they are reflected in the literature. Therefore, society would somewhat be sensitized about the contradictions that have long been existing between the classes and among the various sections in society through the forms of literature than through the writings of historians. That means the people are made conscious of their miserable material conditions of social life through the various genres of literature, which is a form of social consciousness.

A Proposition

The four select novels whose stories are set up in various historical periods creatively but objectively reflected the then-contemporary social living conditions of Dalits with the historical authenticity of the characterization of characters nonetheless the world outlooks and political inclinations of their respective authors were different. While the novels, Untouchable Spring and The Grip of Change have potential to propel people to create a new humane history, the other two novels Untouchable and Sangati remain as the texts that can evoke sympathetic feelings among the people about the miserable plight of Dalits and the Dalit women.

The Glossary

Dalit Panthers: A movement of Dalits that arose in Maharastra in April 1972.

Manu Dharma: The Hindu religious code of conduct

Basava: Founder of Lingayat movement in South India.

Bagotam: Street Play

Malas: Scheduled caste people in Andhra Pradesh

Madigas: Scheduled caste people in Andhra Pradesh

Palle: An area, adjoined to the village, wherein malas and madigas live.

Peddamala: Elder of malas.

Peddamadiga: Elder of madigas

Karanam: Village administrator

Kapus: A land owning upper caste landlords

Reddies: A land owning upper caste landlords

Choudaries: A land owning upper caste landlords

Gandhiji: Father of Nation, India.

B. R. Ambedkar: A great Dalit leader and crusader of his community.

Surasura Puranam: An epic of gods and rakshasas

Rakshasas: Native people of India but they are considered evil by Brahmanists.

Ganga: The goddess of water and considered the mother of Rakshasas.

Brahma: The creator of the world according to Hindu mythology.

Urumula dance: A folk dance which is usually performed by Dalits.

Chenchu Lakshmi: An incarnation of goddess Lakshmi according to Hindu mythology.

Rayalaseema: One of the regions of Andhra Pradesh.

C.P. Brown: A broad-minded British officer who worked for the development of

Telugu language.

Vemana: A progressive poet of the 18 th century.

Periyar: He is a social reformer and philosopher. He led the self-respect movement in Tamil Nadu against Brahminical domination.

Jyotirao Phule: He is the father of the struggle to abolish casteism in Maharastra by fighting against brahminical domination.

Dvipadas: Couplets in Telugu language.

Lone Star Mission: In Nellore region, the American Baptist Mission began under the name, Lone Star Mission.

Bhagavatam: An epic which narrates the miracles of lord Vishnu.

Potuluri Veerabrahmam: A sage in the 17 th century in Telugu society. His teachings endeared him to Dalits and other lower castes.

Gangiregu: A tree which is widely grown and seen in Andhra Pradesh.

Namu: Grain loan.

Geviti tree: Neem tree.

Ooru: Village

Bhadrakali: A goddess and ferocious warrior and consort of Lord Veerabhadra according to Hindu mythology.

Kali: One of the incarnations of goddess Parvati according to Hindu mythology.

Bairagi: A saint

Poleramma: One of the incarnations of goddess Parvati. Goddess Parvati incarnated 101 times according to Hindu mythology.

Komaraiah: A peasant and revolutionary in Telangana region before Independence.

He was killed by the landlords. He was the first martyr in the peasants' struggle against Nizam's feudal regime in the erstwhile independent state of Hyderabad.

Mantras: Chanting of Holy lines from ancient scriptures

Agama Sastram: The code of Hindu religious principles that should be followed by Hindus.

Tonga-Wallah: The driver of a horse-driven carriage.

Panchayat: Local administrative body at village level.

Ramayana: It is an epic and holy book of Hindus.

Mahabharata: It is an Itihasa and holy book of Hindus.

Eley: Addressing and ordering people with authority and also with disrespect.

Sami: A polite way addressing the elders and high ranked persons.

Ayyo: An interjection. It is used when one is shocked or hurt.

Deepavali: A Hindu religious festival.

Pongal: A Hindu harvest festival.

Scheduled Castes: Depressed castes in India.

Padayachi: A backward caste.

Reddiar: A land owning caste Hindu community.

Cheri: An area adjoined the village wherein the scheduled castes live in.

Chakkiliars: An aboriginal agricultural community. They work with leather and are considered untouchables.

Parayars: An aboriginal agricultural community. They were forced to do menial jobs like scavenging, burning the dead etc., and are considered untouchables.

Tahsildar: Revenue officer at block level.

Thatha: Grandfather.

Vesti: A garment which is worn by men. It covers the body from waist to feet.

Production relations: Property relations or social relations.

Productive forces: Land, tools, equipment, labour etc., which are required for production.

Production system: Both production relations and productive forces are together are called the production system of a country.

State: A country considered as an organized political community controlled by one government.

State machinery: The institutions such as police, courts, jails etc., which help the Government rule the people.

State violence: Violence by the state-run institutions i.e. state machinery.

Classes: Groups of people in a society that are thought of as being at the same social or economic level.

Class struggle: Struggle between the two main classes--exploiters
and the exploited.

Bourgeois (adj): Supporting the interests of capitalism

Bourgeoisie (noun): The capitalist class.

Naxalism: A Revolutionary Communist Political Thought.

Naxalite: A person who believes in Naxalism.

Karl Marx: Proponent of the dialectical and historical materialism and founder of scientific socialism.

Frederic Engels: Close associate of Karl Marx and one of the proponents of the dialectical and historical materialism and founder of scientific socialism.

V.I. Lenin: Russian Communist Revolutionary and a great exponent of Marxist philosophy.

J.V. Stalin: The President of the U.S.S.R. after V.I. Lenin and an exponent of Marxist philosophy..

Mao: The Chinese communist revolutionary and an exponent of Marxist philosophy.

Simone de Beauvoir: French writer and Philosopher (1908 – 1986)

Works Cited

Primary Sources

Rao, Kalyana, G. Untouchable Spring. Trans. Uma Alladi and Sridhar I. New

Delhi: Orient Black Swan Pvt Ltd publication, 2010. Print.

Sivakami, P. The Grip of Change and Author's Notes. Chennai: Orient

Longman Pvt Ltd publication, 2006. Print.

Anand, Mulk Raj. Untouchable. India: Penguin Books, 2001. Print.

Bama, Sangati (Events). India: Oxford University Press, 2005. Print.

Secondary Sources

Agarwal, Beena and Neeta. Contextualizing Dalit Consciousness in Indian English Literature. Jaipur, India: Yking Books, 2010. Print.

Prasad, Kalekuri. Dalita Sahityam [Dalit Literature]. Guntur, India: Dalita Stree Sahitya Parishat Publication, 2000. Print.

Lunacharsky, Anatoly. "Theses on the Problems of Marxist Criticism". Trans.

Y.Ganuskin. source: A. Lunacharsky: On Literature and Art Progress

Publishers, 1973; Trnscribed by Harrison Fluss for Marxists.org. Feb. 2008. Online.

Marx, Karl and Engels, Frederic. On Literature and Art. Moscow: Progress Publishers, 1978. Print.

Kutty, Govindan P. Marxist philosophy: An Introduction. New Vistas Publications, 2002. Print.

Rao, Varavara, P. Telangana Liberation struggle and Telugu Novel

- An Analysis of Relationship between society and Literature. Hyderabad:
Swetcha Sahiti Publication, 2007. Print.
Rao, Varavara. Bhoomitho Maattaadu, Fiction and content Analysis. Hyderabad: Yuga publications, 2005. Print.
Ranganayakamma, Muppalla. For the solution of the 'caste' question Buddha is not enough, Ambedkar is not enough either, Marx is a must. Trans. B.
R. Bapuji. Hyderabad: Sweet Home Publications, 2001. Print.
Rao, Padma Katti. Dalitula Charitra [History of Dalits]. Ponnuru, Andhra Pradesh: Lokayuta Publications, 2008. Print.
Rao, Padma Katti. Ambedkar, Marx, Phule – Tatvika Samalochanam [An Appreciation]. Ponnuru, India: Lokayuta Publications, 2008. Print.
Ilaiah, Kanche. Mana Tatvam -- Dalita Bahujana Tatvikata, [Our philosophy – Dalit Bahujan Philosophy]. Hyderabad, India: Hyderabad Book Trust, 2000. Print.
Kher, Dhananjaya. Mahatma Jyoti Rao Phule. Trans. Vijayabharati, B. Hyderabad, India: Hyderabad Book Trust, 2010. Print.
Marx, Karl and Engels, Frederic, Manifesto of the Communist Party. Hyderabad: Visalandhra Publication House, 1997. Print.
Sardesai, S.G. and Bose, Dilip. Marxism and The Bhagavad Geeta. Peoples Publishing House (P) Ltd. New Delhi. 2002. Print.
Mandel, Ernest. From Class Society to Communism, An Introduction to Marxism. Published by Venkatarangaiya Foundation. Print.
Rao, Madhusudhana, Tripuraneni. Kavitvam – Chaitanyam [Poetry – Consciousness]. Andhrapradesh: Virasam Publications, 2006. Print.
Gopal, Venu. N. Navalasamayam, Critical Essays and Reviews on Novel.
Swechcha Saahiti Publication, 2006. Print.
Gopal, Venu. N. Four Essays on Post Modernism. A Swechcha Saahiti Publication. Print.
Soma Sundar, Avantsa. Keratalu – Kiranalu [Brief Profiles of

Prominent Writers in the World]. 2007. Print.

Rao, Venkateswara. R. Sahitya Tatvam [The Phylosophy of Literature].

Visalandhra Publishing House, Hyderabad. Print.

Murthy, Bala Rama, E. Bharatiya Tatvam [Indian Philosophy]. Visalandhra Publishing House, Hyderabad. Print.

Devi, Siva Rani. Premchand's Life. Trans. Sita Devi Vasireddy. Print Ranganayakamma, M. Capital Parichayam [An Introduction to Capital]. Sweet Home Publications, Hyderabad. 2004. Print.

Tarakam Bojja. Dalitulu – Rajyam [Dalits and State]. Hyderabad Book Trust, 2008. Print.

Rao, jr. Parsa Venkateswar. "Emancipation Through Artistic Flight."Rev. of Untouchable Spring. The Book Review 34. 10 (Oct 2010) : 30 -31.

Kalaichelvi, P. "Ships and Harbours Subaltern Voices in Tony Morrison's Sula and Sivakami's The Grip of Change."Indian Research Journal of Literatures in English 1.1 (Jan – June 2009): 1- 15.

Nayar, Pramod K. "The Politics of Form in Dalit Fiction: Bama's Sangati and Sivakami's The Grip of Change."Indian Journal of Gender Studies 18.3 (Oct 2011): 365 – 380.

Ray, Arunima. "Caste, Gender and Dalit Women's Discourse of Difference: Reading Bama's Sangati and Sivakami's The Grip of Change."Journal of the School of Language, Literature and Culture Studies 15 New

Series (August 2011): 58-65. [Special Issue on Dalit Literature].

Hornby, A. S. Oxford Advanced Learner's Dictionary, sixth edition, Oxford University Press. Print.

Websites Viewed

www.viewpointmag.com

www.marxists.org/archive/lunachar/1928/criticism.htm

www.marxism.org.uk/articles/3724

www.ambedkar.org

www. Dalitchristian.com

www.varavararao.org

www.ranganayakamma.org
Socialist Realism, From Wikipedia, the free encyclopedia
 Marxist Literary Criticism, From Wikipedia, the free encyclopedia
Dialectical Materialism, From Wikipedia, the free encyclopedia
Historical Materialism, From Wikipedia, the free encyclopedia

www.ingramcontent.com/pod-product-compliance
Lightning Source LLC
Chambersburg PA
CBHW050332160726
48002CB00001B/278